Hamlet of Morningside Heights

Hamlet of Morningside Heights

By

Kenneth Craven

CAMBRIDGE
SCHOLARS
PUBLISHING

Hamlet of Morningside Heights,
by Kenneth Craven

This book first published 2011

Cambridge Scholars Publishing

12 Back Chapman Street, Newcastle upon Tyne, NE6 2XX, UK

British Library Cataloguing in Publication Data
A catalogue record for this book is available from the British Library

ISBN (10): 1-4438-3343-6, ISBN (13): 978-1-4438-3343-1

FOR ROSANNE

Contents

FOREWORD

ANDREW GURR

Kenneth Craven has led a remarkable life, as a lifelong student of Shakespeare and much else. His book records his experiences, entwining its account with references to the work which sustained much of it: *Hamlet*. Paul declared in Romans 12 that God said "Vengeance is mine," and while many commentators on the play have invoked this apparent biblical denial of a son's right to avenge the murder of his father, nobody beside Dr. Craven ever studied the way that the rest of Paul's epistle affects the play. It has staggeringly wide-ranging implications, many of which are identified in this account of how and when these thoughts resounded in Dr. Craven's mind.

Revenge is basic to human interaction. From the malevolent curse or *maleficium* that early witches tried to inflict on their enemies, revenge has always been the first reaction of the weak when oppressed by the strong. Authority hated rebellion, whether by individual assassins or by witches raised in a folklore that they thought gave them power to avenge their grievances. Every individual who makes an attempt to challenge the ideas of order and justice by which members of society tried to claim what they felt were their natural rights, however just or unjust they might be, has its appeal to that innate sense of the unfairness of things that depends on the feeling that revenge can be justified as a response to inflicted injustice. Paul in Romans 12 overrode that feeling. In setting his version of Christianity against such a natural and instinctive impulse, Paul generated vast debate. In the process his version of the loving God stimulated that extraordinary array of plays analysing the conflict between revenge and the alternative responses to it which started with Kyd's *Spanish Tragedy* and found in Shakespeare's *Hamlet* the most sophisticated elaboration of it that we have.

Describing himself as a "Renaissance New Yorker," surrounded by such distinctive life experiences as a brother who designed the Polaris missile, this fascinating personal history of one man's intellectual and academic life through the second half of the last century starts with the famous words of wisdom that Polonius gives to his son in *Hamlet*. Citing

Shakespeare's parody, his many misrepresentations of the commandments that Paul revised in his epistle, and finding them to be texts urged on young American students, Dr. Craven develops a remarkably wide-ranging survey of his and our mental experiences over the last half-century. His journey is full of stopovers that many of us will find familiar, while his readings in *Hamlet* itself will provide a quite different kind of refreshment from those that we usually look for in our stopovers.

—Andrew Gurr

PREFACE

As every reader knows, our particular fate or fortune on every occasion depends on who is busy setting the authoritative rules for whom. When a classic masterpiece like *Hamlet* lays out the limits of our ethical choices, however, time and place can treacherously rewrite the script on right and wrong and who's in charge. Time has inadvertently revised Shakespeare's satirically unsurpassed codification of Old World vices into an opportunistic program of New World virtues based on global empire building. Herein is my detective story on neglected values in the play *Hamlet*. This book considers how time-changing agendas and humane values in governance and learning have reduced individual autonomy in the here and now, even while seductively providing greater authority to a new elite. It is also my personal story told in intimate fashion based on my insider experience of New York executive power.

I am not alone. In 2002, Simon and Schuster published *The Silent War: The Cold War Beneath the Sea*, the distinguished autobiography of my younger brother, John P. Craven. John was the U.S. Navy's chief scientist in the design and implementation of the Polaris missile and submarine, our principal nuclear deterrent and first line of defense in the Cold War. Because his life was surrounded with national secrets, however, he was restricted in what he could say about his private life. At that time, he asked me to describe my own career development more intimately in the corporate and learned worlds. A more revealing picture would thus provide a fuller understanding of our formative years during the Depression and further informed by the rich maturing experiences growing up in New York's unique environment of executive power.

As humanist and Kremlinologist, I, too, made an innovative national contribution to the Cold War. In redressing the Western space imbalance following *Sputnik* in 1957, I was co-director in creating the first schools in information and computer science and developing their doctoral curriculum for a new breed of information scientists at the behest of the Federal Government in cooperation with the *Fortune 500* corporations and the National Science Foundation. In my further career as corporate consultant for infrastructure, I was influential in the planning and implementation of new procurement strategies at AT&T and in developing the organizational structure of the City University of New York.

In 2006, the second edition of my *Jonathan Swift and the Millennium of Madness: The Information Age in Swift's* 'A Tale of a Tub' analyzed John Locke's conflicting New World legacy of popular sovereignty and colonial slavery. As an intellectual historian since 1982, I have lectured at University of London and contributed to numerous international conferences and learned societies in Europe on the Enlightenment.

My advisory team has worked unstintingly in converting a strictly business professional into a conversational storyteller. My wife, Rosanne, has provided balance, wisdom, hard truth, and the constant North Star love Shakespeare calls for in Sonnet 116. My depth editor, Jean Longfellow, since 2001 has already published 50 volumes of Minnesota Law. She, too, has never shirked in her tough love in telling the author to drop his generalities and to place his occasional golden sentences and stories into prominence. Michael Clinton, my friend and AT&T colleague since 1975, has been a partner in writing on the rise and fall of AT&T. Having both management and board of director experience, Michael has kept my writing on New York executive power raised to the policy and planning levels.

Since my 1992 lecture in London on quintessence in *Hamlet*, Andrew Gurr has left no stone unturned in his searching critiques of my scholarship. We share mutual enthusiasm and commitment for discovering and preserving the hard-won truths based on verifiable records of Shakespeare's canon and milieu. Given the higher dimensions and elegance of Andrew's work on Shakespeare, I am humbled to have his guidance and endorsement in the foreword of this book.

Helen Dos Santos has served since 2009 as copy editor and production assistant in publishing this book. Her up-to-date computer expertise has made up for the technological shortcomings of the author. Even more critically, her artistic flair and younger contemporary perspective are evident in the unique jacket of the reproduced 1585 map of Elsinore. Every team should have a closer who arrives to judge that the totality and details of the entire project are done and done. Alicia Nadkarni, former editor of a university press, has arrived in timely fashion to perform that function.

CHAPTER ONE

HUMANIST

As humanist and career insider in New York's major centers of executive power on Wall Street, Greenwich Village, and the theater district, I have worked alongside a galaxy of America's finest leaders. They fashioned themselves as quixotic self-made heroines and heroes dedicated to causes, visions, and dreams; they fought *avante garde* and rearguard for good against evil using the enabling virtues of faith, hope, love, justice, fortitude, prudence, and temperance while shunning the vices of lust, gluttony, greed, sloth, wrath, envy, and pride.

We all lived, however, in a pragmatic century defined by widening genocide and wars. Coordinately, the American masses had been enticed into unrealized fantasies, leading to increasing drug and gambling addiction, and new levels of violence and prisons. Amidst this unrelenting onslaught of evil, goodness retreats, overmatched by the new lures of fortune. If Don Quixote has been satirized since the beginning of the seventeenth century for lack of realism in the modern world, where then may humans turn next to instill the 7 virtues over the 7 seductive vices?

I bring to the table executive experience in both the corporate and learned worlds. In both the Depression and Cold War eras, I either immersed myself in New York industry or in learning, graduating from Columbia College on Morningside Heights in 1949 and from Columbia University with a PhD in 1967. Consequently, I have observed the daunting ethical problems of modern urban culture with two different sets of spectacles. I follow on the heels of William Shakespeare who similarly looked at the hero of the modern world with both commercial and learned eyes.

Literary and psychological critics from Ivan Turgenev in 1860 to James Shapiro in 2005 have contrasted the active goodness of Quixote's satirized and waning chivalric tradition fighting evil at large with the introspective skeptical analysis of Hamlet, the rising hero. Hamlet is southern Quixote's northern replacement, who fights against evil for the communal soul at large, but first attends to his own soul. Through soliloquies introduced for the first time in the 1600 *Hamlet*, Shakespeare has his hero weigh the scales of good and evil by examining his own consciousness. In a now "distracted globe" (1.5.98. Quotations come from David Bevington and David Scott Kastan, eds. *Hamlet, Prince of Denmark*. New York: Bantam Classic, 2005), Hamlet's soul seeks out those blessed few like the classic Horatio, whose sanguine psychic humor and tutored judgment resists becoming "passion's slave" (3.2.71), that plaything for Fortune in our descent as "a pipe for Fortune's finger" (3.2.69). Either examine your soul and love your neighbor or follow fickle Fortune and beggar your neighbor. Human choice is reduced to two ladies. "Since my dear soul was mistress of her choice" (3.2.62) distinguishes Hamlet from the toadies around Claudius who obey in lock step the self-degrading "strumpet Fortune" (2.2.493).

Thus, the priority of personal salvation first replaces the white knight's honor to save the victimized. Shapiro, as we will see, credits the 1580 secular essays of Michel de Montaigne as initiating this new leadership trend of self-examination. This innovation of self-knowledge prefigures a major systemic change in European leadership. The northern migration of this new direction by way of *Hamlet* into the English and Russian novel and psychoanalysis has been my major lifelong professional and personal concern. Whether called the soliloquy, the interior monologue, the digression, the dialectic of the soul, stream of consciousness, or the unconscious, these revelations have become the defining moments in the novels of James Joyce and in my eight-year study of psychoanalysis. I am alert to these leadership nuances and history in both allied disciplines. There is, however, ironic development in two opposite directions. Even as these rigorous developments in self-knowledge have dominated intellectual life since Shakespeare, the new masses have been treated to information overload in pursuit of fortune. Having careers in academia and Wall Street has allowed me to monitor these contrary spiritual and material developments.

In these disciplines, I have been blessed with mentors. As to the literary origins of this new introspection, like Shakespeare in 1599, at age 24 in 1946, I became attached to the stylish essays of Montaigne in translation: Shapiro's original innovator. I had come under the strong skeptical influence of Donald Frame, the world's leading twentieth-century authority on Montaigne. From 1946 until 1949, Frame served as my close undergraduate advisor; he was also my professor in four honors colloquia limited to fourteen chosen upperclassmen in the Great Books at Columbia College on Morningside Heights. Like me, Frame, too, fully adopted many of the open-minded, skeptical ideas and the restrained and balanced peaceful psyche of his sixteenth-century model, Montaigne.

Yet, like Shapiro, I have my own fully-documented original source for revealing the model of Hamlet's soul-searching inner being. At the time of the play's composition in 1599, Elizabethan popular literature featured the self-examination of the melancholy St. Paul and the psychology of humors. Not only were Paul's mood-driven swings recognized at the center of the Elizabethan public consciousness, but John Calvin's heavily-dependent Pauline works and the 1572 Bishop's Bible further extend the ubiquity of Paul's spiritual experience as a role model throughout that century of religious fluctuation. Romans 12–13 which depends on "renewing of the mind," encapsulates Paul's entire credo of ethical precepts. As I discovered, these Pauline principles permeate Hamlet's psyche from the stymie at every turn of "outrageous fortune" (3.1.59) until he recognizes, like Paul, the limitless possibilities for guidance in the providential design of "a divinity" (5.2.10). This new light on conscious self-knowledge in literature, life, and psychoanalysis brings my work together with the 2005 work of Shapiro on Montaigne (*A Year in the Life of William Shakespeare: 1599*, Columbia University Press) and Stephen Paul Thompson's generally ignored and thoroughly informed 1990 University of Iowa PhD dissertation, "Shakespeare and the Elizabethan St. Paul." My own balancing contributions are revealed here for the first time on Shakespeare's intricate appropriation of Romans 12–13, chapter and verse, as the ethical touchstone on four counts throughout *Hamlet*—two satirical and two at the core. We have here a half century of my combined literary detective work finally coming into focus.

In 1953, I had already discovered the inventive self-serving revision of the Pauline source in Polonius's ridiculous wise saws in *Hamlet* that provided a parodic field day on the old man's cultural and spiritual blindness for Shakespeare, his hero, and the Elizabethan audience. Polonius's debased template for upward bound youth on every count specifically denied Paul's parallel codified credo in Romans 12–13 of love thy neighbor, by endorsing instead beggar thy neighbor. The sacrificial heart of the Christian faith was thus traded in for the callous heart of seeking pragmatic fortune.

I may be the first, but I am not the only scholar to recognize that Shakespeare uses allusions from Paul that Elizabethans would easily understand. In the year 2000, without knowing about my own comparable, unpublished 1953 find linking *Hamlet* with Romans or Thompson's 1990 dissertation, the academic Steven Marx published *Shakespeare and the Bible* (Oxford, 2000), a little book about *The Merchant of Venice*. In it, he shows how Shakespeare had cleverly utilized St. Paul's Epistle to the

Romans in the New Testament in the same way that Paul had prepared his New Testament epistle by writing over the Old Testament Mosaic Law.

It was in graduate school at Columbia in 1953 that my Sunday school lessons as a child sunk in. They were reinforced on the well-to-do Methodist side of Division Avenue and the daily family Bible readings on the poor Puritan side of Division Avenue where we lived in Brooklyn, New York. They combined to lead me to make this first of four vital connections between Romans 12–13 and *Hamlet*. The other three are the oft-questioned satiric Reynaldo scene (see chapter eight), the soliloquies as Paul's key recommendation as the means for a dedicated leader to discover divine providence (see this chapter and *passim*), and finally, the biblical defense of a new Christian revenge tragedy (see chapter ten).

In uncovering the original biblical source that Shakespeare and believing Elizabethans relied on, I ultimately identified the single thread that runs through the entire play *Hamlet.* The soliloquies of the main character match the critical spiritual decisions of my own life. *Hamlet*, utilizing Paul's summarized values and convictions, gives full scope to the tragic and comic arguments for either loving or exploiting one's neighbor. There is no middle way.

The final three connections came in this century. Together these four discoveries, at last, establish Romans 12–13 as the executive key of the play *Hamlet*. These two New Testament chapter references are used satirically at the expense of Polonius. Yet, at the same time, these two key chapters define Hamlet's mission. Thus, at once, we are finally led into the dialectic mystery that undergirds the thoughts and actions of the central character and the contemporary belief system and the plot architecture that binds the play together. Ironically, all four references would be recognizable in the Elizabethan public domain, while they are increasingly removed from ours. What the four references say about the mystery of my own life and perilous times are just as critical as they also serendipitously uncover for the reader and me the foundations of my own leadership credo. Thus this detective story connects the profound mysteries of the play with my life.

Until now, however, like others, I had missed the true reading of Paul's sublime leadership principles in *Hamlet*. The Elizabethans, unlike us, knew all about St. Paul. These principles assumed philosophical importance in the 1590s by felicitously joining the humanistic Renaissance with the Protestant Reformation, syncretic Middle Eastern classical and religious juxtapositions from Shakespeare's era. From crossing Division Avenue in New York, I could finally see the "fell [mighty] opposites" (5.2.61–62) in leadership between the character Polonius, a stand-in for Lord Burghley, and Paul played out across time. Burghley served as chief overlord for Edward, Mary, and Elizabeth, the three reigns of Henry VIII's Tudor offspring in the sixteenth century.

If modern audiences and scholars have missed satire on Polonius's wise saws, they have also missed satire's obverse side: the serious cumulative use of Pauline ethics at the heart of the play. If finding the Paul-Polonius disconnect is brand new to modern consciousness, then reading on will further jolt received opinion because Paul's Romans 12–13 goes deeply to the mystery of the play. What Polonius, Fortune's slave, rejects, Hamlet, Paul's disciple, ultimately accepts. While Polonius displays woeful ignorance of Paul's Christian ethics, Hamlet stumbles on the heart of Romans 12–13 through his inner dialogues and his own precipitous actions.

Thanks to humanism, the plot of classical revenge tragedy has finally assumed a Christian ethical dimension. But there is one key passage from the beginning of Romans 12 that determines the character of Hamlet, the structure of the play, and its central mystery: my major discovery about Pauline ethics in the play and self-discovery in this book. Since nonconformity wins out over earthly fortune, the two verses became my guiding light, as it became Paul's and Hamlet's, as a result of examined experience.

> I beseech you therefore brethren by the mercifulness of God, that ye geve up your bodyes a quicke sacrifice, holy, acceptable unto God, which is your reasonable service. And be not ye fashioned lyke unto this World: *but* be ye changed in your shape, by the renuying of your mynde, that ye maye prove What is the good, and acceptable, and perfect Wyl of God (Rom. 12:1–2, emphasis added. I use the 1572 Bishop's Bible throughout).

This biblical quote puts the whole good and evil counterpoint of the play in motion. If humanism in its encompassing ethical focus incorporates noninstitutional Christianity, so Paul's passage on the ultimate Christian duty can just as easily apply to all humanism's scorn of unethical fortune. Shakespeare, through invoking Paul, captured a wide audience interested in values then and now; from rabid Puritans like my father to humanists like myself. You don't have to be Christian to accept Paul's credo.

After all these years, I finally see that my soul has been living permanently in Shakespeare's London (1592–1616). I gravitated to this post-Renaissance era because my father put me there. As I did not qualify as one of the Elect who would go to heaven, my rigid Puritan father had uncannily laid out a decidedly secular role for me within this earlier transitional time and place. Traditional institutions of church and state had been shaken, but no new empowerment centers had yet risen to dislodge them. Zealous reformers anxious for systemic change of all political, economic, and cultural continental landscapes on a global, colonial scale still required the entire seventeenth century to overcome monarchical tenacity. I happily embraced Shakespeare's time and priorities.

My father infallibly labeled me as a secular humanist yoking classical and Christian thought, well before I had heard of my fellows like Dante, Ficino, Erasmus, More, Rabelais, Cervantes, Shakespeare, and Montaigne. Like Shakespeare's contemporary Earl of Essex, a model for Hamlet, my passions ultimately became delicately attuned to the divine harmony of William Byrd, the rollicking romp of the madrigalists, and the melancholy humor of doleful John Dowland. Meanwhile, my conscience responded to St. Paul's simplification of Mosaic law—love thy neighbor rather than exploit her—while my new found consciousness of skeptical introspection was activated by Montaigne and John Donne. Both my father and my unconscious assigned me to this major commercial and learned urban habitat, London. New York and London have since been my stages to become an authority on a half millennium of radical changes in the "outrageous fortune" of a less than brave New World (3.1.59). I staked out those Elizabethan and Jacobean periods (1558–1625) when America was merely a glint in merchant adventurist and Puritan eyes, the bloody religious 30 Years War (1618–1648) had just begun, and the new Great Britain was still a quarter century from beheading Charles I in 1649. After that, much that was new, both good and bad, languished on the sidelines in Britain until William and Mary in 1688.

Situated in the twentieth century, my father believed deeply the hollow American dream sequence: God had ordained this new Garden of Eden for Puritans, His elected surrogates. A born contrarian, I didn't believe that Reformation prophecy so I was more than a little underfoot at home and in public. Meanwhile, as the centerpiece in my father's profound national credo, my brother John, the second male heir, would handsomely consecrate this sacred American turf in the twentieth century by fashioning military arms to hasten this blessed country's global manifest destiny. John rose as the undisputed chief scientist in development of both the Polaris submarine and Polaris missile: the nuclear shield. Michael Clinton, my close friend of over thirty years, who has read books by and about my brother's brilliant career has accurately captured these parentally-designated diametrical life missions: "John had that rare capacity to solve the most daunting known technological problems facing our survival in the twentieth century, while Ken, on the other hand, laid out the most daunting humanistic problems with mature clarity that the war-ravaged twentieth century has been too preoccupied and too proud to face, such as unclear nuclear misdeeds that have at last crowded in upon us" (personal communication with the author). Thus, my father's clashing wishes have come true.

Columbia College, the colossus on Morningside Heights, is at the center of this book that simultaneously connects the profound meaning of my own life of vast horizons with Shakespeare's play *Hamlet*. The historical pathway to negotiating long-range change is my business and the play's constant theme. Thus *Hamlet* illuminates the interconnected foundation of my two interlocking careers as a consummate systems analyst and active broker of major change in the corporate world. I am also an accomplished intellectual historian and observer on the premises in tracing continuity and change in learning, commerce, and governance from the Renaissance to the Information Age.

Modern change has featured increasing new mass forms of slavery, penury, murder, destruction, and terror. All global empire building, including our own, rests on manipulating these economic priorities at the expense of humanistic ones. Only if one has concentrated on these emerging global evils masked as pragmatic human improvement can one contribute to the cause of the good. These fabulous interconnections between operational evil and poorly matched good could not be juxtaposed without four deeply-researched landmark studies analyzing millennial change that serendipitously corroborate each other. One milestone connects *Hamlet* with these vast changes. The other three landmarks examining earthshaking new directions in human society are mine.

In the 2005 edition of the remarkable *A Year in the Life of William Shakespeare: 1599*, the first landmark, James Shapiro, chair of Shakespearean studies at Columbia, concentrates on the profound system-wide changes in Europe reflected in the 1599 *Hamlet*: the death of chivalry, fading Catholicism, and the rise of global capitalism. The combined thesis of our corroborative research would be that *Hamlet* at the tipping point registers on both sides of these dramatic new directions in European governance, religion, learning, and culture. Shakespeare does this by contrasting a discredited chivalric tradition, linked to honor, to the rising power of the British merchant class, linked to that "strumpet Fortune" (2.2.493)—that is, to self-degradation—and equipped like the Dutch to explore and exploit investment in the New World. Writing *Hamlet* in these changing times, Shakespeare abandons the theses of his history plays. He also rewrites the traditional well-worn plots of classical revenge tragedy to concentrate on salvation, the individual's psychological struggles, and on Paul's Christian revenge instead of honor. He does so by using brand new soliloquies characteristic of Montaigne's essays and St. Paul's Epistle to the Romans. As for capitalism, these earliest Dutch-English commercial investment initiatives, including a 1624 stock exchange, gained momentum and are still alive on Wall Street today and embedded in my commercial ancestry.

Shapiro has rung the changes on every important new light on *Hamlet*, including his own critical discoveries and their meaning. There is, however, a central clue of historic European change that I discovered and he missed running throughout the play and the modern era. I established this discovery with Oscar James Campbell, his predecessor at Columbia a half-century ago, that validates our similar theses, and that receives here the first full light of day to complement and build on Shapiro's own revelations. In 1953, I realized that the revered wise saws of the old fool Polonius were a gross misreading, a witty parody of St. Paul's ethical principles. Paul reduces his spiritual principles to the daylight metaphor of love thy neighbor, while Polonius reduces his selfish maxims to the night metaphor of exploit thy neighbor, by fashioning a modern calculated material self. A half century later when I returned to the play, I realized an epiphany: the *Hamlet* plot and character revolve around St. Paul's own melancholy life and principles set forth in Romans 12–13. Gross changes engineered on a macro level require individual changes in ethics and personality for which Shakespeare sets down his ideal against new synthetic reforms.

Complementing Shapiro's 2005 landmark, my own three landmarks update and confirm Shakespeare on the knell of historic systemic change. My rare interlocking learned and corporate careers feature profound systems analysis throughout my life. That is, I have specialized in intellectual history of human watershed changes. In addition, I have joined my expertise on systems analysis with the executive role of negotiating broker in corporate America to institute the best of these irrevocable changes smoothly among ultimate winners and losers. Thus, my three published landmarks deal with further European dystopian and utopian change in the 1690s, 1950s, and now.

Recently, the Afterword of the 2006 reprinted second edition of my globally-reviewed *Jonathan Swift and the Millennium of Madness: The Information Age in* 'A Tale of a Tub' (E.J. Brill, 1992, and iUniverse, 2006), my own first landmark, looks ahead of the 1599 *Hamlet* after one revolutionary century in flux to the stabilizing 1690s. In that pivotal decade, the philosopher-executive John Locke, a systems analyst and brilliant sleight-of-hand broker of change was the most influential high commissioner of British trade and colonial empire building. The good and bad changes he brokered then in economically crippling Ireland and the colonies featured violence and slavery and the pursuit of other intangible property that permanently impaired his conflicting ideas of democracy and human rights. The powerful Locke, having set the new world on its irrevocable two-way ruinous course, left future American leaders with the impossible systemic task of breaking his contradictory, but now ossified elitest bonds ever since.

Reformers of global change like Locke run up against the realities of stubborn traditions and these elitists often languish in the wings of power, at home and abroad, for decades waiting for that fortunate break like the installation of William and Mary in 1688. Once a frustrated new elite finally arrives, however, they quickly institute long term policy changes in science, economics, and culture like Locke's early mercantilism in the interest of the public weal. Meanwhile, these global innovators exhibit no remorse for victims of a new poverty or concerns for a new admixture of virtue and vice, and act without a scintilla of humility.

My second landmark, the co-authored 1961 *Science Information Personnel: The New Profession of Information*, (Modern Language Association and National Science Foundation), triggered by *Sputnik* in 1957, brought about systemic change in the organization and doctoral education of science information globally. We discovered that key humanistic and notational knowledge systems and their ethical principles had been systematically excluded and shelved in seventeenth-century Europe by the new empiricist elite of the Royal Society. Bad decisions made by European scientists three centuries earlier came home to haunt the West in the space race in 1957. These major losses in other knowledge systems were replaced by measurable experimental science serving narrow pragmatism and economic utility. In fact, European scientists and political world changers dominated radical reforms at the expense of humanistic knowledge and the liberal arts. In this one unanticipated global crisis, we redressed the space and systems imbalances in 1961 by reconstituting knowledge and language losses from the seventeenth century that the Russian Academy of Sciences had not neglected.

The ebb and flow of the seventeenth century between old political, economic, and cultural traditions in Europe and novel permanent global replacements indicate Shakespeare's prescience in seeing the systemic conflicts in the offing between old and new ethical and knowledge systems. Thus, this book on *Hamlet*, my own third landmark, describes further deterioration in our time of waning viable knowledge systems and peaceful virtues amidst the rise of uncontrolled economic empire building, fortune seeking, and global exploitation. Situated simultaneously in the

1599 world that created *Hamlet* at the budding of modern culture and in 2011 at its failed global resolution, I have been able through these four landmark studies to pinpoint the critical moments of cultural deterioration. The tide of vicious new systems with all-powerful technological and economic tags for an elite has swamped countervailing humanistic answers.

These four learned researches including this initial 2011 volume thus rest on the sweeping systemic changes in seventeenth-century Europe consummated after Shakespeare's recording years. They anticipate the current global systemic change in governance, commerce, and culture defined by that centuries-earlier upheaval. They also reflect the totality of my life horizons developed in New York and designed to identify and resolve these systemic crises in this century.

Without institutional dedication to either a single religious faith or economic belief system, I enjoy the luxury and obligation of observing my multi-dimensional universe within this wider humanistic focus. Skeptical of any psychic health in the modern ethos, I have crossed all "the Division Avenues" of rich and poor cultures; I have studied Shakespeare under leading authorities and seen productions of his works here and abroad from the 1940s, when I was in my twenties, to the present. I have taught the entire Shakespeare canon in six full-year courses at three major universities, at both undergraduate and graduate levels, between 1955 and 1973: West Virginia University, Rutgers University, and City College of the City University of New York. I also find the Bard not singularly focused. Where are his identifying cross, flag, and economic icons? In vain, scholars and advocates have tried to pin down firmly-held allegiances for Shakespeare, but the many points of view in his plays cancel each other out by their sheer multiplicity. He has remained dedicated to universals detected in particulars, while prescribing no simple formulas or panaceas, and functioning best in the public domain, or what was called the *consensus gentium*, that is, what we all say amen to without needing further proof.

As a Renaissance New Yorker, at my own personal level of attainment, I, too, have bridging and observational credentials that function creatively in either the stalls where the elite sit or the pit where the masses stand. Just as a child I crossed Division Avenue in Williamsburg, Brooklyn countless times from the poor to the elite side, so as an adult, like Shakespeare, I have constantly shuttled between the commercial, learned, and corporate worlds and, in that process, between low and high cultures. As a maverick in both ends, I have teetered on that seesaw between the highly competitive business brokerage negotiations of the socio-economic world and the slow analytical processes of the humanistic one, for roughly two-thirds of the twentieth century. I have discovered that each distinct social class and each distinct world looks at those assigned a different lot in life with mixed feelings of curiosity, stereotyping, threat, and vicarious voyeurism. It's why we go to the movies and read the tabloids. In some instances, I have been quizzically wondered about, variously tarred, secretly envied, and fully exploited by opposing camps. Even as I write this, clearly my bridging two classes of society—rich and poor—and two professional worlds—corporate and learned—inhibits my full integration in all four communities.

While my outsider status has ensured elusive independence, autonomy, and unfettered observational outposts instead of pure power, most authorities I served under with excellence hoped eventually, but usually in vain, that I would join their institutional team in some long-term powerful capacity. But I never identified permanently with a single safe controlling environment or faith. Like the world of Tudor London, I think in painfully slow transitions and systemic changes. Looking for stabilizing universals and controlling executive power during transitional periods focuses my perspectives. Sweeping movements and new horizons grab my attention full time.

For example, once the 'brave new world' popped over Columbus's horizon in 1492, the public domain in every field of endeavor changed everywhere for everyone. Monarchs, courtiers, and prelates, the losers, suddenly had to watch their backs as the past was gutted for new precedents to modify and overturn old ways. The resulting new sixteenth-century cultural task was to infiltrate the public domain of medieval Catholicism with new ideas, which were at the ready in the Reformation. The Renaissance, a mother lode from the classical world, also served as a constant reconfirming reference on the true nature of the human condition and the basis for systemic change.

No one in his century was better than the judicious Shakespeare at appropriating and renovating that public domain: using the past in the present to broker and negotiate stable directions and to frame iconic references for future epochs. All publicly sensitive authors, including me, use allusions recognizable to their audience. Trafficking in allusions that were established in the public domain became his franchise where he stole blatantly from the past, defined the present and contributed fulsomely to the new public domain into our era. His overriding influence on the public domain has been so pervasive that imperishable characters he created as heroes or villains have become icons for their traits. Or they were even recast in opposite new roles, as we shall see, where their vices, for

Elizabethans, have been transformed to virtues, to conform to the mores of a new "distracted globe" (1.5.98).

The great contribution of what we now call the Renaissance, was that all the great human developments of the ancient Middle Eastern and African classical worlds finally became wedded to the medieval Christian world picture. With Columbus, the New World in particular became the new testing laboratory for old and new systems. Neither belief systems nor their delineating partner, drama, escape this literal transitional sea change. For whatever it was worth, the tree of knowledge of good and evil gave forth both new fruit and serpentine pestilence in the new Garden of Eden, America.

My father recreated his Puritan New World in the twentieth century, and Shakespeare, as you would expect, was even more alert in creating vivid images for his Elizabethan audience of the prospective new public domain, that Garden of Eden, in America. Exactly one century after Columbus, Shakespeare anticipated the golden promise of the exotic New World enticingly and staked out his own claim there. He hardly short-changed his audience, then and now. Fortune became the overriding new lure, allusion, and illusion in every direction. Virtue took a back seat to temptation for everyone. In his early play, *The Comedy of Errors*, he describes America as embellished with rubies and sapphires.

Shakespeare's glancing references throughout his plays to the West Indies, South Sea discoveries, Indians, new nations, enchanted isles, and the expanding globe itself piqued his diverse audiences' private expectations of new vistas just opened to each and every one. But even his idealized world of *The Tempest* has serpentine torments. Anglican adventurers, merchants, religionists, and settlers from all classes of society finally vied with their monarchs for these new places in the American sun. Tangibly and intangibly, everyone now had a fabulous and uncharted new public domain to dream about, to allude to, and explore with body and soul. As his reward for pointing Europe imaginatively westward, Shakespeare's own status in the American public domain remains secure. Ever since 1492, America, property, William Shakespeare, and the Bible (even though each has been severely re-interpreted) have been closely bound together as the shared public domain of the one, the few, and the many, particularly in the Anglo-American world picture.

Shakespeare gave this imagined new world its dream-like structure; that impending world returned the favor by adopting or adapting his dramatic perspectives into their exciting new public domain. In this transitional environment, Shakespeare simply gave his sophisticated and unsophisticated, Elizabethan urban audiences exactly what they craved in imaginative dreams attainable in new generations. They experienced daily the painful tragedy of enduring the final years of a glorious, but splenetic queen in her dotage. They leaped to the trope of the pleasurable comedy of a brand-new, enabling century that blended a magical providential joined to a secular New World featuring new inventions, discoveries, networks, governance, and learning, and above all, promise of fortune for the newly enfranchised. In all European walks, centuries old inhibitors were being replaced, not without tragic resistance, with promising enablers and some demagogues. In every new appeal of fortune, however, virtues took a pragmatic beating, which Elizabethans realized, while eager modern adventurers discounted virtues at an ethical price.

Luckily, I had Shakespeare's humanistic take on the New World to which I could factor in subsequent, mixed developments. There was one major systemic change in the New World he dramatically represented throughout his art that runs counter to my father's American optimism. In an unbroken literary tradition from Homer, Dante, and Chaucer, he challenged new dreams of fortune for everyone, at the expense of established value systems of vice and virtue formerly accepted in the public domain.

Fortune never motivated me, which proved my costly flaw in the modern world. Humane balance motivated me. John and I both moved from our father's extremes of faith to the productive realms of scientific and humanistic reason, respectively. John had faith that his nuclear deterrents provided temporary breathing room to improve on democracy and the human condition. I see that unending global task as far more daunting than he, with the clock still ticking away.

CHAPTER TWO

LONDON TRANSPLANTS

The founding of the New World meant an altogether new clash between the new community's sense of religious mission and the individual's new economic quest for fortune. Consider my father's conflicting priorities of mission and fortune to fit our New World. Similarly, the overarching ideas of the Reformation and the Renaissance clashed in sixteenth-century Tudor England. The rabid Catholic Queen Mary Tudor sent the Puritans, the ones she didn't kill, packing to Switzerland where they picked up revolutionary ideas, missions cherished by both my father and Woodrow Wilson, in hastening the Second Coming and instituting parliamentary civil government. Fortunately for the New World, these so-called Marian Exiles were repatriated by Queen Elizabeth I to become the primary revolutionary force for mission and economic growth in England, America, and Europe against absolute monarchy in the following centuries.

This split between loyalist-royalists and parliamentarians seeped into colonial America and into my branch of the Craven family up to my seventh American generation. In a quirk of fate, my father is the spitting image of the portrait of his distant relative, Sir William Craven, Lord Mayor of Shakespeare's London in 1610–1611 and fortunate head of the Merchant Taylors' Guild. My zealous father and the Swiss Calvin remain on the same page of the prophetic Reformation. What's more, our great grandfather, the merchant Tunis Craven, one of the wealthiest men in Brooklyn Heights in the nineteenth century, consciously emulated the Lord Mayor's Anglican lifestyle to a tee, just as I followed in the footsteps of his contemporary Shakespeare from that same period. The real life parallels between the two fortune seekers—the rich Lord Mayor and his doting American heir, Tunis—are as incredible as my re-creating my life vicariously in Shakespeare's London during those same years.

Ironically, my father notwithstanding, Tunis and I enjoy intimate and passionate parallel connections that are longstanding and close. In 1562, thirty years before Shakespeare arrived in London, the fourteen-year-old William Craven, our remote ancestor, walked up to London with cattle drovers, penniless, leaving behind his West Yorkshire family and bleak Craven Dales roots, the locale of *Wuthering Heights*. He was apprenticed to a mercer, a dealer in textiles, in the Merchant Taylors' Guild in the city until he reached his majority in 1569. By employing the same kind of commercial spirit and diligence in the textile business as Shakespeare did in the entertainment business, he, too, rose to wealth and honor as one of the richest men in the newly created Great Britain.

On Queen Elizabeth's death and his accession to this expanded empire in 1603, James I, the first of the heavy-handed, botching Stuarts, in the interests of preserving their shaky rule of one, wisely accepted Shakespeare's company as the King's Men and, at the same time, knighted the wealthy Sir William Craven. Along with the Earl of Craven, his namesake son, this invincible mayoral ancestor loyally contributed thousands of pounds, infinitely more than any other merchant family, to prop up the deservedly ill-fated Stuart Crown until their very last day on the throne when the beleaguered James II fled to Catholic France in 1688. Nonetheless, like Shakespeare remembering his provincial Stratford roots, this other London success story, Sir William Craven, the widely philanthropic father, endowed Burnsall, his rural Yorkshire birthplace, with a school, a refurbished church, and a causeway to his village, Appletreewick.

This fortune-seeking Craven family urge to trade rural rags for urban riches and civic honor has left permanent marks on succeeding generations, particularly evident when Tunis tried to replicate Jacobean London in nineteenth-century Brooklyn, New York. Tunis Craven, my three times great grandfather, had this same merchant class sense of invincibility.

Tunis was the grandson of Thomas Craven (b. 1709), an impoverished London East Ender, a scrivener's son from Spitalfields outside Bishopsgate. Thomas came to Philadelphia and the Pennsylvania Plantations in 1727 at age 18. He paid for his transatlantic passage by serving five years as an indentured servant in Bucks County, Pennsylvania. Following servitude, the scholarly Thomas ended up in scholarly penury, a British royalist schoolmaster in Hunterdon County, across the Delaware River from Pennsylvania, in what was then the West Jersey colony. In the mid-seventeenth century, Jersey was a colony split down the middle between royalists and revolutionaries. This split occurred even within his own family. While Thomas and his wife lie buried in a neglected and isolated royalist graveyard, no bigger than a front lawn, in Ringoes, New Jersey, their twelve sons and daughters went on to believe in the American Revolution.

Grandson Tunis Craven fashioned his own Anglican-Episcopalian Garden of Eden in Brooklyn, and hated the Puritan branch of the family. He also rejected the schoolmaster role of his grandfather Thomas and modeled his life strictly on Sir William Craven, the fortunate London Lord Mayor from Shakespeare's time, two hundred years earlier. Through diligence and keen dealings, he became a wealthy coal merchant in Virginia, married the daughter of Commodore Thomas Tingey, head of the Washington Navy Yard, and, in consequence, later enjoyed a successful, mercantile career in charge of purchasing all naval stores for the Brooklyn Navy Yard in the second quarter of the nineteenth century. That's good fortune. He was, in his era, the Navy's one-man Pentagon procurement office for all naval stores from coal to cooperage.

Tunis used the 1610 Mayor's family seal and crest in all his business dealings. The Lord Mayor of London still reigns in the commodious Mansion House today. In replicating his ancestor's authority, opulence, and residence, Tunis erected his own luxurious Mansion House in 1826 on Hicks Street in Brooklyn Heights, with 126 windows—an indication of its immensity and prestige. Before it became an elegant hotel, he raised three invincible sons in grand heroic British style there: one became an admiral, whose ship, aptly-named Brooklyn, was responsible for the burning of New Orleans; another died in battle; and a third son served as chief engineer of the Croton Aqueduct and the entire New York City water system as it currently exists. While his ancestor and heir served a king patriotically and philanthropically in London, Tunis and heirs also served their new Eden patriotically and productively in New York.

Ultimately, like my strictly business, nineteenth-century great grandparent, I, too, made my own destiny reliving that transitional past. I immersed myself in the life of the merchant Shakespeare as a bridging male model just as Tunis had with Shakespeare's contemporary and his mercantile ancestor, the Lord Mayor of London. Upward-boundness with allegiance to both high and low cultures has always been a family condition. So has cross-cultural marriages into other European traditions added spice to our now nine American generations. To me, Shakespeare provided a humanistic survival kit against ubiquitous tyranny that everyone on both sides of Division Avenue, sooner or later, faces personally in everyday life. His Elizabethan and poetic vocabularies and his high-low bordering lifestyles became part of my autonomous tool kit, even while first serving at the level of impoverished schoolmaster in Burlington, New Jersey, thereby retracing the footsteps of my first American grandfather Thomas.

Because we returned to the past, Tunis and I have well-worn, marked cards in our deck. If you hung out in the Elizabethan and Jacobean public domain like Tunis and I did, you served your apprenticeship to the protocols, civilities, values, convictions, and genius of that period. You learned your way about the City of London town ringed around by political, economic, and social authority, but looking for autonomous breakthroughs, like the clever slave of classical and Elizabethan dramas. Nonetheless, we two were and are, still very much at home in the American present because that Eurocentric, commercial-cultural world continues to dominate. The past did not run away and hide. The past made my present a success. Since my Columbia PhD in 1967, the traditional haunts of Oxford, London, and the United Kingdom as archival treasure still draw me for about one month every year. Our modern life is still run with similar feudal and hierarchical controls in church, state, and commerce in both English-speaking societies.

The universals in our human nature and its institutions don't change that much. Authority's controls have not changed much either. That's certain. New technologies just give them a sharper edge. If you know this truth, you have more to go on in circumventing institutional authority. I rose high and served long as a consultant on infrastructure for AT&T in the 1970s because I had learned the perennial laws of medieval feudal hierarchies during five years studying the identical patterns of the Soviet secular priesthood at Columbia's Russian Institute and the Renaissance hierarchies earlier in its Faculty of Philosophy. These longer-term, historical perspectives on life, human nature, and power served me well. In a word, contemporary fashions sooner or later become assimilated into the long-term continuity of the universal human condition. If that continuity did not continue to control things behind the scenes, classical drama, Shakespeare, and the hierarchical merchant class—offshoots of the medieval guild system—would not still appeal, serve as touchstone, and make money; they would now be merely anachronisms.

CHAPTER THREE

ELIZABETHAN VICE AS AMERICAN VIRTUE

If I have literally transplanted myself to Shakespeare's London, it stands to reason that my understanding of Shakespeare's canon and the Elizabethan world picture will match neither Shakespeare, his works, nor his time as they are customarily re-interpreted in our own transitional era. My intimacy with Shakespeare begins with a particular feature of the Renaissance and the developing New World: expanding and exploiting the public domain. Understandably, Shakespearean scholars often miss the Bard's merchandising skills. Understandably, both America's flourishing Garden of Eden and Shakespeare's overflowing art could not have succeeded without appropriating from others.

The public domain, however, is a mixed bag of properties, not always used in a good cause. Some call it stealing. Indeed, how could anyone ever flourish without all that property, real and intangible, handed down to all of us in the public domain? The public domain, an essentially American legalism, basically establishes free use of lands or property unclaimed under American law. The new public domain features fortune at the expense of virtue. For example, through four centuries, this great American freedom or hubris, gave us permission to commit genocide on the Native Americans and enslave Africans as property in the name of Christianity and trade, and atomize the Japanese for treachery so that servicemen like me could cut short our overseas tour of duty.

Intangible property, too, has been subject to appropriation throughout history and now on the ubiquitous Internet. Without constant allusion to a wide level of common knowledge accessible in the public domain, all artists would have difficulty reaching audiences. William Shakespeare had the best knack for borrowing and adding to the public domain. The dramatist had no equal in stealing private property and reallocating it to the public domain where he could make a lot of money. In his business, he had to cross Division Avenue in time and in his own place, continually, in order to appropriate recognizable particulars from any quarter. All Elizabethan playwrights raided ancient, medieval, and contemporary sources and materials without a "by your leave." Shakespeare proved to be by far their preeminent, finest, and most copious borrower of other dramatists' public property. Why not? His allusions and metaphors packed them in. Possessed of the rarest integrating imaginative process, every tremor, every particular of his time and time past was grist for his mill. Even the play *Hamlet* borrows from an original from the Middle Ages and allusions from another produced ten years earlier, but now lost. By transforming recognizable particulars to universals from seemingly disparate sources, Shakespeare became for his contemporary audience the most complete renovator of the public domain then accessible on the cusp of the equally transforming Elizabethan-Jacobean reigns from 1558 to 1625. He evoked among his contemporary audiences the affirmation that this is what we know and now see in a new and clearer transforming light about virtue and vice. I, too, used my passion, flair, and merchandising background in concert with acquired classical learning to interrelate amongst the one, the few, and the many, also expanding my own public domain wider than my peers. Instinctively, I, too, saw America in that new public light of choosing virtue or vice.

In borrowing from the public domain, one doesn't always get it right. On what constitutes secular moral behavior, Shakespeare has been widely misinterpreted in the public domain of American education. Ironically, Shakespeare's immense American legacy ever since colonial times, runs almost completely against the grain of our parallel cross-cultural life journeys. That trans-Atlantic legacy, principally the seven tragedies—*Julius Caesar, The Merchant of Venice, Romeo and Juliet, Hamlet, Othello, Macbeth*, and *Richard III*—continue to thrive in the American public domain as an Anglo-American institution, theatrical, and scholarly industries and, above all, as an elite-controlled secular ideology on an influential par with the Bible. The pithy epigrams, epitomes, metaphors, stock characters, and situations have been required reading in far greater than half of all American public, private, and parochial high schools for almost a century, despite ideological fashion changes.

Hamlet was required study for all American high school seniors for most of the twentieth century. They usually also had to memorize the selfish maxims of the grasping old fool Polonius where personal aggrandizement, that is, making one's fortune is gospel. It was a national requirement. I had that assignment in 1937 and my wife Rosanne had it twenty-two years later in 1959. Every good, ethical American was told in high school not only to take Polonius at face value, but to revere him in Shakespeare's hallowed name. Polonius had misunderstood and reduced to a hilarious viciousness a familiar biblical passage of virtuous maxims Elizabethans knew, venerated, and memorized. As we will see, what was his contemptible vice and advice to the Elizabethans became the height of virtue and selfish individualism in the thoughtless public domain of American public education, fortune hunting, and board rooms. Elizabethans would have been dumbfounded that this scheming villain had become the exemplar for a whole nation of psychically disordered adolescents. American society got good and evil, salvation and fortune, and cultural balance and imbalance reversed.

How did this all come about? Let's now suppose that Moses, St. Paul, and Shakespeare's Polonius have a three-way conversation intended to rivet and to convince Eurocentric audiences. The conversation starts when Moses descends from the mount with God's Ten Commandments. Most of us remember the ones about adultery, honoring our parents, and staying out of jail. Paul, however, thinks that he can improve on the Mosaic Law by reducing all God's commandments to one, without checking with God, of course. The result is numerous epistles on Christian behavior and their justifications. But in Romans 12–13, Paul has attempted to codify the basic Christian laws, just as the Ten Commandments codify the Hebrew religion. A few understandable basic principles in one key accessible place make it easier to figure out what God, ethics, and the society wants us to do every time, every day, rather than trying to figure the laws out one at a time, on a case-by-case basis. Wanting to have Christianity in a simple package, Elizabethans, and many other Christian cultures before and since took Romans 12–13 to be the Christian credo and lifestyle in a nutshell. Paul intended that. Immediately after reducing Christianity to a few prescriptive rules, paraphrasing Paul in chapter 13, verse 9 of Romans: if I've overloaded you with all these letters, here's all you have to do. In the Elizabethan's Bishop's Bible, his take-one-pill-a-day version reads, "And if there be any other commandment, it is in fewe wordes comprehended in this saying: Namely, Thou shalt love thy neyghbour as thee selfe" (Rom. 13:9). Clear enough—make no distinction between loving your neighbor and yourself.

That's fine until Shakespeare's revisionist fortune hunter Polonius came on stage. Both Old and New Testament summations of ethical laws work for the common good leading to goodwill, harmony and peace. Meanwhile Polonius operates with his own selfish set of values based on the world of appearances. The play's entire infrastructure depends on the tensions between Paul's Christian ethics and Polonius's philosophy of self-reliance leading to personal wealth, inequalities, and power contests. The priorities uppermost in these diametrical belief systems set up a constant counterpoint between the fierce opposites of good and evil, soul and body, divine grace and fickle fortune, love and exploitation.

Shakespeare sets these two systems in stark relief with one of the most precisely constructed and brilliantly imagined parodies in drama ever. Elizabethans would have gotten his allusions and seen the contrasts. Moderns do not because they are afflicted culturally with the value system and fashionable world of Polonius that Shakespeare parodies. Since the play pivots on the success of fortune hunters over the soul searcher Hamlet, Shakespeare parodies their reverse ethics by having Polonius read and bungle and twist Paul's credo. It is Shakespeare's dramatic triumph that in the very act of stumbling through and distorting one ethical system based on the Christian sense of community, his elitest villain can depict its reversal. By instinctively substituting for each communal recommendation of Paul his own personal system praising the transparent opposite value of rugged individualism without ethics, he places all emphasis on fashion and the outer man.

Polonius is no incidental character, but is modeled after Lord Burghley who was chief counselor in the three Tudor regimes of Edward, Mary, and Elizabeth after the death of Henry VIII. As we shall see later, these were his own personal self-aggrandizing values codified for his sons as delineated by his biographers.

Let's set the scene. Polonius's son, Laertes, Hamlet's friend, can't wait to board a boat for libertine Paris. He has just given his sister Ophelia an unsolicited lecture on how to fend off Hamlet's guaranteed sexual advances (1.3.1–51). According to Laertes, the prince has royal lust on his agenda, free of all complications. Ophelia pointedly asks him if he can take his own advice, a challenge that only makes him readier to hop on board for lustful Paris. But at that inopportune moment, the tedious Polonius hastens on stage and forestalls him in just the nick of time. Laertes must endure, like all American high school seniors, listening to the wise saws of his boring old father delivered as gospel. To back him up, Polonius has his thumb on chapters 12–13 of Romans and opens his Bible to them. Like other advice givers, he wishes to legitimize his own precepts based on a revered text. But his ethically informed Elizabethan audience soon learns that obviously he has not looked at these biblical precepts in their public domain previously, and when caught on the spot, he hastily garbles them so thoroughly that they precisely match his own selfish philosophy of life: winner-take-all. By the time he gets to the end of chapter 13, verse 9, he has revised the Christian credo just as thoroughly as Paul revised the sacred Hebrew Ten Commandments, in the same manner, in the same epistle.

As an immediate confirmation of the parody, both Paul and Polonius conclude their diametrical ethical creeds with identical metaphors, the same ringing endorsements and confident, pithy conclusions. If there's one commandment that sums up my exhortation best, it's love thy neighbor, says Paul. No way, says Polonius. Exploit thy neighbor: "This above all: to thine own self be true" (1.3.78). The parody of their conclusions is even keener as they use the same night and day metaphor, but in reverse. After all his exhorting in these chapters, Paul is well spent but has just enough oratorical juice left to come up with the typical "born-again" dawning light so hoped for by evangelical Christianity later: "The nyght is passed, the day is comme nygh. Let us therefore cast away the deedes of darknesse, and let us put on the armour of lyght" (Rom. 13:12). Polonius, on the other hand, has garbled Paul's text and *ad libbing* comes up with his own rhetorical flourish at the end, reversing Paul's glorious born-again day for his inky night as the final resting place of his philosophy: "And it must follow, as the night the day, / Thou canst not then be false to any man" (1.3.79–80).

In addition to the transparent textual evidence above and below, we have external evidence from the earliest printed quartos, the form of Shakespeare's published works, from prompt books. In Quarto 1 (1603), we find quotation marks on every line of the old fool's precepts, but nowhere else in that text and removed in all subsequent printed editions. I came across the reference to Polonius holding the book prop in a remote quarto, after Quarto 2 (1604/5), about half a century ago.

Once you know Shakespeare's original source, the parallel internal textual correlations are delicious reversals. Let us consider Paul's emotional, communal order to "Rejoyce with them that doo rejoice, and weepe with them that weepe" (Rom. 12:15). We've all heard that. The cautious Polonius will have none of these excessive outbursts: "Give thy thoughts no tongue, / Nor any unproportioned thought his act" (1.3.59–60).

Next, Paul wants his followers to mix with all walks of society. "Beyng of lyke affection one towardes another, beyng not hye mynded: *but* makyng your selves equall to them of the lower sort. Be not wise in your owne opinions" (Rom. 12:16, emphasis added). In other words, cross Division Avenue. Polonius wants Laertes to pick and choose his contacts among the elite; affection doesn't enter into it. The 22-floor Yale Club opposite Grand Central terminal in midtown New York would be just fine. Try getting past the front door. He says, "Be thou familiar, *but* by no means vulgar" (1.3.61, emphasis added).

Both Paul and Polonius warn against picking a quarrel, but with the 'but' they again part ways. Paul: "If it be possible, as muche as lyeth in you, lyve peaceably with al menne. Dearly beloved, avenge not your selves, *but* rather geve place unto wrath" (Rom. 12:18–19, emphasis added). Polonius wants Laertes to mix it up, if he has to show his manhood: "Beware / of entrance to a quarrel, *but* being in, / Bear't that th'opposed may beware of thee" (1.3.65–67, emphasis added). Don't strike first; that's stupid. Everyone else and their brothers will come after you. But jolly well retaliate. Paul asks the Christian to turn the other cheek: "Blesse them whiche persecute you, blesse, and curse not" (Rom. 12:14). According to Polonius, you don't reach out to either friend or enemy. Just keep your mouth shut. "Give every man thy ear, *but* few thy voice; / Take each man's censure, *but* reserve thy judgment" (1.3.68–69, emphasis added).

When it comes to the body, they couldn't disagree more. To Paul, fashion the body as a sacrifice to God. To Polonius, fashion the body as a clotheshorse to the latest modes in Paris. Paul:

> I beseech you therefore brethren by the mercifulness of God, that ye geve up your bodyes a quicke sacrifice, holy, acceptable unto God, which is your reasonable service. And be not ye fashioned lyke unto this World: *but* be ye changed in your shape, by the renuying of your mynde, that ye maye prove What is the good, and acceptable, and perfect Wyl of God" (Rom. 12:1-2, emphasis added.).

God has nothing to do with it for Polonius. Laertes must only stay in tune with Parisian fashion. Polonius:

> Costly thy habit as thy purse can buy,
> *But* not expressed in fancy; rich, not gaudy,
> For the apparel oft proclaims the man,
> And they in France of the best rank and station
> Are of a most select and generous chief in that.
> (1.3.70–74, emphasis added)

If you're into making your fortune, nothing's changed. Join the discriminating elite.

Paul teems with generosity and love while Polonius is tight-fisted and selfish. Paul: "Owe nothing to no man, *but* to love one another" (Rom. 13:8); "Distributing to the necessitie of saints, geven to hospitalitie" (Rom. 12:13); "Therefore, if thyne enemie hunger, feede him: if he thyrst, geve hym drynke. For in so dooying, thou shalt heape coals of fyre on his head" (Rom. 12:20). Opting for the main pragmatic chance, Polonius sees owing simply as a cash proposition. Polonius: "Neither a borrower nor a lender be, / *For* loan oft loses both itself and friend, / And borrowing dulleth edge of husbandry" (1.3.75–77, emphasis added). As for husbandry, Paul will have none of it. Even if one belongs to the elite, open barns and wells; even to enemies, even at a cost.

If Paul in Romans rewrote the Old Testament to knock it over, I discovered a half-century ago that Shakespeare rewrote Paul's essential two chapters from Romans (12–13) in *Hamlet* to have Polonius deny everything that Paul proposes about Christianity. Yet these are the essential chapters on ethics that every good Elizabethan Christian, Protestant, and Catholic, or even millenarian evangelical, should know, particularly if they're pressed for time. True, it might have been difficult when Elizabethans had to apply this love thy neighbor across the board to Anglicans, Puritans, and Catholics. But that commandment remains the Elizabethan equivalent of the American Pledge of Allegiance. Why is Shakespeare, or more specifically, why is one of his vicious characters denying the basic tenet of every Christian, both now and then? And how did growing up in Brooklyn give me this insight?

There is grave irony here. Again, detectives perk up their senses when there are incongruities. Secular ethics that dominate the American public domain fly directly in the face of the spiritual dimensions of the Pauline ethics. Thanks to *Hamlet*, Shakespeare expected the secular ethics he satirized to be deliciously savored in the Elizabethan public domain as rebellious opposition to dominant Pauline ethics. Little could he foresee that these satirized ethics articulated by the fool Polonius would become secular gospel for worldly success for generations of Americans from day one, or that they would be officially authorized because they carried his play's internal sanction. The turn-the-other-cheek Pauline everyday ethics for Elizabethans would be exchanged for Polonius's to-thine-ownself-be-true everyday ethics by Americans. The Pauline centerpiece is the communal command, "love thy neighbor," while Polonius's centerpiece is the individual's looking out for oneself. What's more, this very passage became the one text that American high school seniors had to memorize during most of the twentieth century as great moral truths. Polonius concludes, "This above all, to thine own self be true, / And it must follow, as the night the day, / Thou canst not then be false to any man" (1.3.78–80). To skeptical me, this maxim for succeeding in the American way of life—which is indeed one tried and true way in a pluralistic society—was pure balderdash. Throughout the play, Polonius is most true to himself when he is duplicitous, and therefore, false to every Elizabethan man, woman, and child who took in the play. I was not to be easily taken in like other educated Americans by this non-ethical, destructive point of view. Gospel to American educators was façade, selfishness, and deceit to this contrarian.

Had American culture become so depraved and the national educators of ethical values become so cynical as to pass off selfish exploitation of others as Shakespearean wisdom? In our vaunted pluralistic society throughout the twentieth century, American secular beliefs were being inculcated just before the senior prom at the expense of American sacred beliefs. Do your own thing, and by anyone's ethical definition, you will fit in. Standards be damned. And where were the Shakespearean scholars, here and abroad? If we go Polonius's way, who is left with a discriminating mind to protect American democracy from demagogues? I knew something was wrong with Polonius's precepts from a Christian point of view when I was in high school; they had actually misrepresented the Bible.

I certainly didn't know at that time that Shakespeare had three other more serious references; one satirical and two about sacrificial leadership dependent on Romans 12–13, at the heart of the mystery of *Hamlet*. Polonius denied Paul and the Christian faith. For me as a Brooklyn teenager, I was not into the meaning of this difference. I would learn. One system of the fool must have been off-the-wall to the funny bone of his Elizabethan audience; but that system had become American basic faith three and a half centuries later.

For another example, among high school seniors in the 1960s, Fortinbras, which means literally "strong in arms," the military adventurer in *Hamlet*, became a casualty of the calamitous Vietnam War where we, too, over-reached and over-killed. But fashionably, among seniors in the 1990s experiencing the Desert War, Fortinbras was greatly rehabilitated for exhibiting far more decisive action than the melancholic intellectual Hamlet and for his youthful readiness to take over-aggressively what didn't belong to him.

Shakespeare as an American institution and industry also functions full time. Why wouldn't modern audiences adapt Shakespeare to their shifting public domains? Likewise, Elizabethan audiences had their own priorities and burning issues that dominated their public domain, and the dramatist would not disappoint them. As time goes by, an enduring past gem gets appropriated by the ruling elite, the learned, and theatrical producers. The resulting complications from trying to relate that audience's public domain with ours inevitably lead to reductive interpretations in two ways. Either we factor out what the present wants the past to be, or we restructure a past object within current existing issues and philosophical constructs. Off in a closet, succeeding generations of academics laboriously tease out particular strands. From time to time, one or another of these sources has become a breakthrough or the latest fashionable avenue for scholarly exploration. Even actors often see *Hamlet* as a new interpretive vehicle to top off a brilliant career.

But Shakespeare as an American ideology, institution, and industry is not my Shakespeare. I am a unique cosmopolitan, an interdisciplinary intellectual historian, a broker of systemic change. As a merchandiser and classicist who has also spent an entire lifetime crossing each and every Division Avenue I could find, I relate to the marketing and classical Shakespeare in a far more unique way than his and my contemporaries, whom he and I often vex. To live intimately among various classes in society without joining them is to observe objectively and understand how they interact and interrelate. This rare bird perch provides a unique opportunity to observe objectively the cultural architecture of an era and its evolution over time. On this level, I have felt that the classical dramatist and I have been on speaking terms–often to the consternation of the learned and political worlds that re-interpret him at a personal and professional distance. The universal, nonetheless, remains a constant. Consequently, anyone attempting to know my cosmopolitan world must know Shakespeare on my multicultural urban terms, and vice versa. Understanding our journeys richly illuminates Shakespeare's contrarian life, and mine.

Raiding the wider public domain or not, you don't enter London, someone else's backyard, unannounced, to scavenge without making enemies. In 1592, when the twenty-eight-year-old Shakespeare, who had come from Warwickshire, made his mark in London as a mere common actor and playwright without a university background, he was pilloried by Robert Greene, a long entrenched rival playwright. Greene was one of the university playwrights, who as a privileged group, wanted to send this rural commoner back to the sticks. Greene's envious tirade referred to this bombastic provincial upstart, a jack-of-all-trades, as a Shake-scene, a tiger's hide, and one who struts like a crow. Implicit in Greene's mixed metaphor invective was the perception that this highly conceited common actor-playwright promoted a sense of his own invincibility and excellence, rode rough shod on a fast track, and borrowed copiously from his peers. Finally, he had no compunction in rearranging the hierarchical status quo in governance, the theatrical community, and received opinion in the public domain. He wielded the executive power described in this book.

Surmounting such fierce envy, the plague, and competition, his career played out according to plan. Six years later, this proud executive Shakespeare, as business director of The Globe at Southwark on the Thames, was entitled to 10 percent of the profits of his acting company, the Lord Chamberlain's Men. The company had already performed before

Queen Elizabeth, then in her last years; the dramatic poet would soon have a court patron and friend in the Third Earl of Southampton among the disaffected oligarchic few; and he had an established reputation for legitimate business dealings and pleasurable performances among the applauding many. As a businessman more successful than his father, he could retire by 1613 in good health and spirits, well before his fiftieth year, to his birthplace in Stratford on the serpentine Avon, having amassed a huge estate to pass on to his heirs. By trade, he belonged to the common culture, but by skillful intermixing of both low-brow popular and high-brow classical dramatic sources, this commoner introduced his public and aristocratic audience to their inevitable interaction, and in the process, was awarded elite status in public life and universal understanding, while living and dead. This intertwining describes my Renaissance approach to navigating and creating a life in New York.

How then does one mine for the universal in life? Others cross Division Avenue physically every day. My goal in crossing Division Avenue was to reach prowess and invincibility by suppressing completely personal concerns and advocacy, to attain the universal. The one at the apex of a pyramid can, in addition to assimilating particulars, avoid personal advocacy and transform them to universals. For example, without choosing sides, Shakespeare squelches both Puritans and idlers in the play *Twelfth Night* by having the idler Sir Toby Belch write off the Puritan Malvolio: "Dost thou think, because thou art / virtuous, there shall be no more cakes and ale" (2.3.107–108). Likewise as a psychotherapist, I would have immediately broken for good the painstakingly-crafted therapeutic alliance if I had just once introduced either a personal note or one judgmental commentary into even one dedicated session. The more the analyst and the reluctant analysand concentrate on the latter's painful particulars, the greater the emergence of an assimilating *gestalt* and a realistic universal backdrop. From a further perspective, the consummate gift of the four geniuses of European humor—Rabelais, Cervantes, Shakespeare, and Sterne—was to present both the finite great and finite small as ridiculous against the background of the infinite: parochial particulars fading in light of the real universal.

His fiercest rival, Ben Jonson gave Shakespeare the greatest universal accolade: "not of an age, but for all time" (Jonson, 1623). Fortuitously, their time was propitious for casting off the past and adopting newness. As Hamlet says, in the age, "the toe of the peasant comes so near the heel of the courtier" that it hurts (5.1.140–41). Both Great Britain and European civilization were at crossroads. Shakespeare thrived in London at the end of the sixteenth century, while all his countrymen, on one hand, could not wait for the demise of the lingering Elizabeth, who had become an ever increasing menace in her oppressive declining years, and, on the other, for the golden promises of America that their Spanish rivals were temptingly fulfilling. In the 1590s, Shakespeare's plays illustrated both sides of the pain and promise Elizabethan coin. He was the only playwright of his day to chronicle English history systematically with pointed references against Elizabeth, which she bitterly recognized in the deposed Richard II, and in building hopes for her successor in the guise of Henry V.

Thus, at the very time that a future pluralistic, mercantile, chaotic, and technologically dangerous America was being imagined, depopulated of its natives, and restocked with fleeing Europeans and captured black slaves, Shakespeare assimilated and marketed all that reasonable folk reasonably needed to know about the authority-autonomy imbalance in antic human behavior. From a universal perspective, he called what was happening over our millennium this "distracted globe," meaning comically and tragically mad (1.5.98). He even created a Shakespeare industry with dividends still accumulating for his native Stratford that continues to thrive in both our high and low cultures today. If you're going to commute between many worlds in time and space, a consummate poetic imagination will take you wherever you are going. If, by a decree of fate, I, too, have commuted widely, at least, my powers of analysis and survival have been assisted by the Bard's poetic laser beam as a trustworthy guide into the darker regions of our being and this distracted globe.

CHAPTER FOUR

RECKONING FOR OLD FOOLS

In melding particulars into universals as Shakespeare does, I developed a unique specialty: the commonalities of old age. My deep understanding of the circumstances surrounding aging began at Columbia in 1951 when I was twenty-nine and studying the history of drama. Old age can be an infectious lark and/or a grim reckoning. The universal conclusion that it is grim is backed by Shakespeare's final word. Nature's "common theme / Is death of fathers" (*Hamlet* 1.2.103–104). This certain transfer of all property including human within families, communities, and dynasties is the inevitable way of the world. Because death of the patriarchal power activates the seven deadly sins, we learn more about evil than good at this ritual changeover, as witness *King Lear*. Death of fathers is also the entire play's common theme for the character Hamlet and the audience. *Hamlet*, first performed in 1600, is actually about the Earl of Essex, the queen's favorite and former lover become dangerous demon, and the future James I. They were drawn from Elizabethan reality, as both stood in the wings as king-maker or royal candidate awaiting either Elizabeth's deposition or her death, or Essex's decapitation, whichever would come first. Each had impeccable, overlapping credentials as a contemporary model for Hamlet as each had a mother who married his father's murderer.

Since the character Hamlet shuttles between Oedipal and comic fathers, I have had a head start on all other critics of his masterpiece. By the time I taught courses in Shakespeare at the City University of New York in 1968, when I was forty-seven, and had studied psychoanalysis for eight years in the 1970s, I had become the world-class authority on the tragic father, Oedipus, and these comic fathers. I had benefitted immensely from parallels in these two overlapping careers as a scholar studying classical drama and myth, and as a psychoanalytic psychotherapist. No other Shakespearean can make or has made this claim—or wants to. Anyone with a public library card can check out my syntheses of the *Oedipus complex*—an ancient literary and modern psychoanalytic convention—as well as *senex amator*—the dirty old man from ancient times to all times—in two extended entries in the *Dictionary of Literary Themes and Motifs* (Greenwood Press, 1988).

In his plays, the Oedipal and comic old men shared the same fate. Shakespeare's comedic knight, fallen from grace and postponing his own bad news, Falstaff, masterful in high and pop cultures, savored the good life and saw the same humor in all his walks of life. Audiences in all ages would pay anything to see this old man in *Henry IV, Part 2* who was "not only witty in [himself], but the cause that wit is in other men" (1.2.10–11). The Bard, however, simply made Falstaff's ending that much more grim by having his tavern bosom buddy, the erstwhile playboy prince, reject him utterly when he became King, with the words, "I know thee not, old man" (5.5.48).

I learned about the comic father long before I became one and the tragic father even as I was positioning myself for that guaranteed role. It all happened in a haphazard way that I became, and remain, this world-class authority on classical drama. It began in high school when I neglected my studies for the glitter of New York entertainment. I should have realized that I had failed miserably in high school because I couldn't keep my mind and heart off the commercial entertainment industry that flourished in New York. I may have roamed into the field of dramatic arts in grad school as a sleepwalker, but I had already sleepwalked through high school studying New York extracurricular glitzy entertainment.

It wasn't Shakespeare, but it was his category: popular entertainment in the urban public domain. As for the *ad-libbing* funny old men, they dominated the stage, films, and radio that I grew up with during the technological transition of the New York entertainment industry in the twentieth century. The great male comic had the spotlight in the silents, vaudeville, the Yiddish theater, burlesque, and early radio—much of it emanating from the Lower East Side milieu that I traversed almost every day. These interlocking stages produced Charlie Chaplin, Buster Keaton, the Marx Brothers, Jack Benny, Eddie Cantor, W. C. Fields, and a motley collection of comedy teams. Further, my own growing up in Williamsburg replicated the real poverty and rich humor of the Lower East Side across the bridge. We also had in our Pinna family a real live Uncle Eddie, a sometime New York taxi driver and sometime clothing cutter, whose wacky, wicked wit, and spontaneous antics would have given any enterprising, clever slave from Roman comedy a run for his money. The family domain had its own unforgettable and uninhibited character actor.

In lieu of doing any homework during my delinquent five-year high school education in the 1930s, I must have attended the actual production of more New York radio broadcasts than any other adolescent in my generation—at least two hundred. I was simply playing hooky from serious study. Time and again, I saw each of the following in person, among countless others: Ronald Reagan in *Death Valley Days*, Fred Allen, Arturo Toscanini, the Dorseys, Glenn Miller, Spike Jones, and Guy Lombardo and his *Lucky Strike Hit Parade*. We had six movie houses within five blocks of our cold-water flat in Williamsburg, including the Commodore, the Marcy, the Republic, the Old Dump Metro, and the New Dump Playhouse, which I attended on Saturday afternoons to see two features and endless serials for a dime. Entertainment was my home away from home. Plays that led to self-knowledge became my secondary informal education. Plays also ensured that I would be on probation during all my undergraduate and graduate years and in later life, too, playing another game called catch-up.

When I came of age, I moved up my love of playing to the incomparable New York theater district and Shakespeare. Home from World War II in 1946, at age 24, I even saw the two greatest Shakespearean actors of their age in tandem: the riveting Ralph Richardson as Falstaff and the sly Laurence Olivier as Justice Shallow, the dirty old men in the fabulous Old Vic production of *Henry IV, Parts 1 and 2* on Broadway. In his New Yorker review back then, Kenneth Tynan credited Richardson's Falstaff with "the down-at-heel dignity of W. C. Fields translated into a nobler language" (*He That Plays the King*, 49). I, too, saw the resemblance. Further, Tynan judged Olivier's Justice Shallow to be a "crone-like pantomime dame, you might have thought, were it not for the beady delectation that steals into his eyes at the mention of sex" (52). In the 1970s, soon after I had retired from teaching Shakespeare at three major universities, the humors tradition, starring the funny old men, reached its American zenith on Broadway and Hollywood with two continuously sold-out performances on stage and screen of *Something Funny Happened on the Way to the Forum*, an adaptation of a Roman comedy by Plautus, and *Fiddler on the Roof*, both starring Zero Mostel. The public domain never resists funny old men.

CHAPTER FIVE

THE HUMORS TRADITION

My postgraduate education on Broadway from 1946 until 1949, with entertainment luminaries like Arthur Schwartz and Irene Selznick, both consciously and unconsciously led me to enroll in Columbia's practical School of Dramatic Arts in February 1949. At the time, it was far from clear that the path of my wayward non-academic activities would turn into a viable career. I was still a sleepwalker.

In those same years, I was distinguishing myself, although I didn't know the honor bestowed on me, as a prospective humanist in Columbia's two-year honors colloquium in the humanities open to only fourteen selected upperclassmen; meanwhile I was just squeaking by in the pre-med science curriculum. During those undergraduate years, I completely failed to understand the significance of those opposite directions. I was still traveling on automatic pilot. Failure to get into any medical school in 1949, however, sent me reeling in the right alternative direction to Columbia's English Department where their combined master's degree within the School of Dramatic Arts and their own history of drama catapulted me within five years to establish once and for all my own credible niche in Shakespearean studies. My entire career path turned around on the basis of one initial interview on entering graduate school. Ironically, everything I had ever done finally connected and fell into its logical place.

My protracted education on the straying old fool began in graduate school. No other professor than the great Renaissance scholar Maurice Valency could have dispatched me down a career path more knowingly, offhandedly, and speedily, while savoring with internal laughter, the naive joke I then was. I became the dogsbody, a menial, of Valency, a tall and handsome, gracefully aging Columbia professor who oozed seductiveness. He loved a jest and had a low-key air about him. In dealing with the malleable student like me, he became whimsical. All in good fun, he casually on two pivotal occasions gave me my marching orders during my first two years of graduate school at Columbia and thereby sealed my scholarly fate in the direction of classical drama. Before they reached my consciousness, Valency saw my parallel affinities with classical drama and Shakespeare; he simply intersected my unconscious and my career by placing these plays before my eyes on a degree requirement basis.

Even before the feminist movement rearranged the male English literature bastion in America, female students flocked to Valency, the true Italian Renaissance man. A master of inner feelings, he exuded supreme superiority and he owned all the necessary props. One of the most brilliant and learned experts on Italian medieval and Renaissance literature from Dante and Petrarch, to Machiavelli and *commedia dell'arte* in his time, he alone among his peers had the appropriate chaise lounge in his office and the ultimate rewarding enticement of a Caribbean villa. He held his Roman toga loosely and would assign anyone to the best role he thought her capable of with offhanded dispatch, humor, and finality. He cut right through to the chase and anything less than compliance he treated as a needless waste of time. None of his graduate students could match his resilience, although I knew one PhD who became mean-spirited and hangdog after years of futile emulation.

Valency had instinctual genius when he had reeled me in originally on a probation basis, solely on a casual, off-the-street interview. After all, I had failed admission to all other graduate schools because of a so-so college record. Stricter scholars and administrators without a sense of humor or humanity or cognizance of my late-blooming Renaissance potential had sent me packing earlier. A year later, Valency proved even more astute on the second interview in assigning me to work on classical funny old men, perennial favorites in the classical and Renaissance humors tradition, with the great dean of Shakespearean scholars, Oscar James Campbell, then in his seventies. Valency assigned me on the basis of my first-year graduate record that otherwise didn't make any sense at all.

Obviously after one year of graduate work, I was still floundering, with no clear career focus. I had had one merchant's foot in Columbia's Brander Matthews School of Dramatic Arts, now defunct, learning how to make it on Broadway with hands-on courses in Shakespeare's jack-of-all-trades repertoire: stage managing, lighting, sets, props, acting, and playwrighting. The other classically-learned foot, I had planted tentatively in the Department of English and Comparative Literature, limiting my scholarly courses to the history of classical drama, Shakespeare's heritage. There I was again between two worlds: merchandising plays or studying the universals in classical drama. I was like Shakespeare operating in two fields, but without any of his consummate credentials or peer rivalries. I was in no way distinguishing myself.

Maybe, some day I could, like the playwright, put these two fields together. As usual throughout my life, my meddling unconscious had taken over, insisting that I be adept at the action of performance and, at the same time, bury myself in the classical closet researching the history of a tradition. Only Valency consciously first saw what my unconscious had in mind. Only Valency, the epitome of the Renaissance New Yorker, could see that I was on the fence between two worlds that my subconscious had already yoked. The aged Campbell was not far behind him in fully exploiting what I had unwittingly brought to the table: commercial and universal perspectives on the drama, a distinctive Shakespearean perspective in the diminished twentieth century.

With flip-flop credentials of his own, Valency became the English Department's matchmaker *extraordinaire*. He speedily diagnosed a graduate student's potential at the end of the first year, chose a fitting master's essay topic, and assigned an advisor. Not shy in feathering his own nest, Valency assigned a number of us to deal separately with each of the stock characters of medieval Italian comedy. *Harlequin*, *Scaramouche*, *Colombine*, *Pantalone*, and *Dottore* had a plebeian history going back to classical Greek and Roman comedy, and a future extending from the fourteenth century to Minsky's Burlesque in the 1930s, which I had sometimes peeked in on on Forty-Second Street, off Times Square. Both the older Campbell and the younger Valency had researched in depth and, accordingly, savored *commedia dell'arte*, the Italian public theater.

Of all the traditions in the theater, none went back farther into public ancient festival or maintained its prominence more securely into the twentieth century than the humors tradition. No tradition depended more on staging and impromptu spontaneity by actors without a script than the humors tradition. No dramatic tradition claimed a stronger affiliation with medical and psychological therapy, harking back to Aristotle, than the humors tradition. After all, I had been a failed pre-med student sadly in need of that psychotherapy. So Valency had saved me on all counts. Why he picked me to trace the dramatic history of these hilarious old men I never knew until this moment. At our determining interview, I encountered the permanent glint in his eye, which I could only match at that juncture with a vacant stare. With characteristic flair, he packed me off to the most elderly professor where the two of us immediately bonded in tracing the inevitable downfall of conniving, meddling, and ridiculous old age.

Somehow Valency saw how hilariously apt—and contrary—it would be to give me the master's essay topic of *senex*, the old man in the humors tradition, and have me work it out under Columbia's *senex*-in-residence.

The septuagenarian Professor Campbell projected a calm equanimity that had been long tested as chairman of Columbia's English Department, by its male *prima donnas*. He had also endured a contentious Shakespearean field that fiercely challenged his authority in print. John Draper, whom we will soon encounter, was a prime nuisance. On another front, he wasted five years writing a book on Italian comedy only to have another formidable scholar, Lily Campbell, unrelated and unaware of Campbell's work, publish a work that made his manuscript redundant. Finally, as an eminent Shakespearean reviewer, he was inundated with, and forced to discard, about one speculative, overblown article or book a month on *Hamlet*.

He knew wheat from chaff. Whether it was the subject of old age and the history of drama so close to his bone, or my conscientious detective work, or obvious scholarly anomaly, Campbell confided in me. Campbell and I bonded more throughout 1952 and 1953 than I did with five other distinguished Columbia doctoral advisors and sponsors through the 1960s. We studied the foolish, harsh, and indulgent fathers, the braggart soldier, *miles gloriosus*, the futile dirty old man, and *senex amator*, in every extant play of Plautus and Terence. We tracked them down as they were passed off as the Italianate *pantalone* and *dottore* in the Renaissance and identified their typical humorous features from Shakespeare's fussy and menacing Old Capulet to Ben Jonson's sly and grasping Volpone. I felt privileged. I felt that this Shakespearean had not met someone earlier who shared his intimacy with the joys of Shakespeare's humor. William Shakespeare, Oscar, and I savored our Elizabethan moment in time on Morningside Heights, New York.

Our relationship did not fit the mentor-disciple or father-son mold, but rather we were secret sharers of the universal humor implicit in old age and the two dramatists who had best rung the changes on it—Plautus and Shakespeare. We had gotten inside the humors tradition, both the medical and literary tradition joined at the hip, bequeathed from Aristotle, Galen, and Plautus to the Elizabethans. While the comedy and the tragedy inherent in the humors were in the extremes of choler, the phlegmatic, and melancholy, the savoring of life and plays about life lay with sanguinity, Aristotle's ideal golden mean. After all the bad news on life had come in, and Campbell had had more than his share, to hold to one's own equilibrium in old age seemed a universal triumph. Shakespearean studies at Columbia on Morningside Heights had a cumulative, exhilarating, salutary effect. Without pointing to it, Campbell brought me into that universal picture in his own makeup and what we shared of the entire medico-dramatic humors tradition, the philosophical underpinning of all great drama. We were a peculiarly matched pair. His challenger Draper, on the other hand, had no facility for laughter, only for the jugular. West Virginia University could do that to you, as I was soon to find out as Draper's colleague.

What makes the old man in the humors tradition funny is universal recognition of the type in the public domain everywhere and forever. Something incongruous takes place as we age and gradually lose it. Part of it is the vain attempts to make the most of any situation, as if the odds weren't already stacked against us as we age. Part of it is the leisure, as in childhood, to return to play and playing, the so-called second childhood, after the adult harness of work and responsibilities. As there are only so many standard plots in life itself, particularly between the generations, so medieval *commedia dell'arte*, that is Italian public theater, had the actors spontaneously improvise on the possible ones constantly recurring and rehearsed in real life.

For example, an old man simulates crocodile tears when he hears of the death of his wife, only to move immediately to spontaneous joy—and carries the audience along with him—when he is encouraged to believe that he now has a real chance to possess his son's new, beautiful young lover. Caught between knavery and foolishness, of course, it will never happen and the audience waits in anticipation for the dirty old man to fall flat in over-anticipation, over-exertion, incapacity, and futility. It's always a question of time. Is he losing his grip? He will. We all know it. Much of W. C. Fields's humor depended on acting out his hostility at the generation gap: "Anyone who hates kids can't be all bad." In one scene, he quickly looks around to see if he is noticed, then with great self-satisfaction kicks an oblivious little kid. Fields played the old fox who improvised and extricated himself best after a few drinks, but the final humorous denouement in age versus youth situations usually comes with some hilarious "trick to catch the old one." If you've lost your ability to woo, you compensate by becoming a miser with your money. Humorists from Jonson's *Volpone* to the age-denying Jack Benny humorously exploited this last-ditch miserly ploy on the stage: Benny famously recounts a thief who asked him, "Your money or your life?" to which he replied, "Wait a minute, I'm thinking." When we go to the theater, dramatists, and actors alike play on our common knowledge that the fundamental things in life are still the same in all ages and climes. We all live in the public domain waiting for something incongruous and funny to happen. It will.

Down through the ages, the real trick in dealing with old age in life and the play is to transform the menace of knaves into the humor of fools.

That's a universal perspective on old age in life and on the stage. The ancient Saturnine Festival, out of which the communally salutary humors tradition was born, allowed ordinary folk one day annually to depict their reigning tyrannical patriarchs, usually knaves, in roles as fools, thus siphoning off and tamping down natural resentments built up during the prior year against peremptory authority. It's the time-honored ploy of all tyrants. Let the unwashed blow off steam. Similarly, down through the ages, the young savor the laughable illusion of performance in the old. As I had lived all my life with the psychic dichotomies between rich and poor, business activity and learning, so I became an expert on the opposite psyches of youth and age before I was 32.

The same universal public domain exists where you might least expect it. In life and literature, the funny old man has been around since Methuselah, making us laugh and cringe. During World War II, I had met one once, living in a remote aboriginal compound tucked away in a jungle at the foothills of the Himalayas. Dressed in a loincloth and cocking a bamboo hat, the funny old man could no longer catch fish with his bow and arrow. Having outworn gainful employment in the primitive compound, the community depended on him for jokes, silly behavior, and baiting the klutzy young American as a foil for his clownishness. Remnants from a more civilized ancient time, Greek and Roman comedy came up with the harsh and indulgent fathers, who often doubled as old lover of their son's date. These were comic staples that passed through Italianate comedy in the Middle Ages, and neatly crept into the works of Shakespeare, Ben Jonson, Moliere, Mozart's operas, and found a permanent home, on and off stage, in twentieth-century New York for our greatest comedians from Charlie Chaplin to Zero Mostel.

Campbell and I had one shining moment when he joyously confirmed that I had stumbled on the biblical key to *Hamlet*. All this traditional matter on old age was straightforward grist for a master's candidate or a playwright until Campbell and I applied the lens of the humors tradition to Polonius, the old fool and father in *Hamlet*. This father and kingly advisor, a pivotal character in the tragedy, has always been studied in the breach; secondary characters have always lived under the scholarly shadow of Prince Hamlet who was, as he himself acknowledged, "too much in the sun" (1.2.67). Campbell confided that, in his view, through the humorous Polonius, I had ironically detected radiant new light on this most profound of all classical tragedies that convincingly led into the heart of the play's mystery. Although it could be well argued that it might have been dangerous to link an emeritus professor with lessened powers with a neophyte on the subject of old fools, Campbell gave my master's essay high honors and helped me hone my Polonius-related findings, which had his *imprimatur*.

I turned these findings into an article to send to James McManaway, then editor of the *Shakespeare Quarterly*, who guided the journal from 1951 through 1972. The editor sat on the article for two years and then rejected it, returning it to me without a single comment. In retrospect, my unheralded discovery might have given my career a slight thrust then, but this rough diamond needed polishing and encasement in a setting that only time itself could fashion. At the time of its rejection, Campbell had left Columbia; we would occasionally meet and greet on upper Broadway, but our intimate interlude and Campbell himself already belonged in the past.

CHAPTER SIX

CUNNING IN ACADEMIA

My introduction to the scholarly controversies on *Hamlet* had begun with the leading Shakespearean of his era, but continued, by a quirk of fate, with his most dogged adversary in my first university appointment. My depression- and war-delayed career path reached the crossroads in February 1954, at age 32, when I received unexpectedly a mid-year appointment as a lowly English instructor at West Virginia University. I had been in a holding pattern for five years as a middle school teacher, social agency camp director, and Fifth Avenue department store floor-walker to support my Columbia graduate studies. All my talents now suddenly had unbridled scope. Ironically, I was hired at $3,700 per year by a needy chairman specifically for my New York business skills rather than for my Columbia MA as a budding Shakespearean. On my first day in Morgantown, West Virginia, I immediately discovered that these credentials at the New York pinnacle in both commerce and learning would lead to multiple leadership assignments beyond my title. In sum, these privileged tasks catapulted me back to the safe environs of Columbia's Russian Institute in June 1956. Yet each of these multiple university assignments prefigured ultimate achievements.

The WVU English Department was an adversarial hornet's nest, being the legacy of three decades of Depression and war with ridiculously low salaries and few perks. The English faculty totaled 42, mostly talented women and men, some with the PhD, some with no hope of the PhD, resigned to composition courses and saddled with family, debt, and demeaning work with no means of escape. Professors Brawner, Crocker, Draper, and Bishop served consecutive 3-year terms as constantly rotating chairs. During these short tenures, each hired henchmen with permanent allegiance and captivity to that particular chair, whether that chair was in or out of power, or again in waiting. Although no one ever mentioned it, permanent English faculty had names of long obsolete English craft guilds: Foster, Gainer, Coulter, Mockler, and Smith.

From the moment I stepped off the plane, I was attacked and importuned from all factions in the department's hornet's nest. The

English chairman Brawner bombarded me with the only reason he had hired an unneeded faculty in mid-semester. As a service manager, I was considered the ideal hire to return a Christmas gift mink coat to a Pittsburgh department store that his wife felt they could ill afford on a chair salary of $5,000. Fortunately, I knew the retail drill: make your successful complaint to the store's president at the pinnacle. At the same time, I was assigned the required business English course, which would be taught for the first time by a business man and not as a free pass by scholars who doggedly introduced literature instead. The improvement was a real student downer as it removed a laugher course. Brawner's gratitude to me was limited by the few perks he had on offer. Two years after the mink coat episode, he assigned me a section of the Shakespeare survey course, unprecedented for an instructor.

I could not have been more apt for this mink coat initiation into higher learning. Of course, back then the customer was always right, regardless of the facts, and the higher one went for satisfaction, the more likely generous restitution would be forthcoming. From my English MA, I had also learned that Hamlet was an ace at customer relations. He twits the fool, Polonius, who would treat each person according to their deserts, that is, their deserving. "No, no," says the Dane. "Use every man after his desert, and who shall scape whipping? Use them after your own honor and dignity. The less they deserve, the more merit is in your bounty" (2.2.529–532). The old fool thinks Hamlet is a little cracked in love or mourning. But on one level, Hamlet's quote is good merchandising! On a deeper level, it facetiously means love thy neighbor as thyself. The higher one goes in retailing, the more this golden rule applies. Do we need further confirmation?

Shakespeare, too, had to shuttle between actively managing and marketing a theater company, while acting and writing timely plays on the side. A department store president had more honor and dignity, backed by corporate reason too, to act far more bountifully to customers than a mere floor-walker like me. Dictating an immediate letter to a predictably bounteous Pittsburgh store president satisfactorily relieved the chair's domestic travail and qualified me to teach, that is, merchandise, a course in business English. Naturally, I hailed as a godsend for the chair's panicky, but wise, cost decision in the short- and long-term. I also immediately learned about vicious infighting in academia that extended to neophytes as well as principals.

The hornet's nest would sting me immediately upon arrival. My own scholarly credentials were challenged that very first day in Morgantown by one of Brawner's and Campbell's adversaries, the Shakespearean John W.

Draper. He was waiting in the wings. Draper was the most prolific world-class scholar on Shakespeare and was in mortal, protracted, combat with my Columbia advisor, Oscar James Campbell, the revered dean of Shakespeareans in his era. I am sure Brawner knew of this connection through my references and used it as a spiteful intramural sidebar to his primary commercial need. Draper sent two of his younger henchmen to my hotel room to invite me to dinner and to play bridge with him that evening before I knew what would hit me. Fortunately, Ted Ross, already two years on the English faculty and an iconoclast hired from the Columbia graduate student pool like me, got wind of my arrival, astutely looked me up that day and mercifully prepared me, a Columbia kindred soul, for what was in store.

Like me, not a clubbable type or capitulator, Ted Ross had stayed outside the intramural rivalries. A strong, independent mind, he had lost his doctoral status at Columbia by directly challenging his distinguished advisor, Lionel Trilling. He was the lonely sophisticate in this academic wilderness and we bonded immediately. He was a gold mine on the pitfalls ahead.

On that initiation day in higher education, I did something that years later signified that I did not intend, even then, to roam forever in that English faculty labyrinth. To celebrate my new status in the world, I stopped by the local record shop where, in that rare mood of enjoying unhoped for success, I purchased the Victor Red Seal album of Modest Mussorgsky's wrenching Russian opera, *Boris Godunov*, sung by the basso Boris Christoff, and enjoyed reflecting on Pushkin's indebtedness to Shakespeare in the text. After all, only three months earlier, I had been confidently told by a snippy New York educational employment agent that my shaky credentials would never, ever allow me to rise above the private prep school level. At that career stage, except for the lucky commercial break of the rejected mink coat, she might well have been right. The Borises returned me once again to my grandfather Pinna's Victorian parlor and the humanely compelling, deeply emotional commitment of the great Russian operatic basso, Feodor Chaliapin. Chaliapin, like Enrico Caruso and John McCormack, became a great vocal staple of the Victor 78 RPM Red Seal records played continually in every middle class household in the 1920s. One needs models, and in a humdrum, Eurocentric world I latched on to what the great operatic basso proposed: Russian deep, rich sound emanating from the soul, portending life's tragic meaning and our lasting awe. Along these lines, Dostoevsky, Pushkin, Tolstoy, Chekhov, and Solzhenitzyn have ever since energized my soul. The Russian opera purchase prefigured my auditing a Russian language course at WVU and returning to Columbia's Russian Institute in 1956 after two and a half years in the hornet's nest. Little did I realize then, that this spur of the moment incongruous purchase anticipated my ultimate career as a *comparatiste*. Unconsciously, I had already set in motion my next scholarly move beyond the WVU English department. This next stop would be fulfilled on my return to Columbia. The nineteenth-century Russian novel emphasized the same nagging universal spiritual questions, that same dialectic of the soul that consumed Shakespeare and the Elizabethans.

Already, I had a bonanza of new insights into higher education. But after needy Brawner, new confidant Ross, and revisited Russia, there was still the imperious Draper, a natural enemy, to deal with on that evening of the exhausting first day of lasting impressions in Morgantown. Draper, my Columbia advisor's prime challenger and goad, oozed hostility. West Virginia University could do that to you, and as my advisor Campbell's disciple, I was about to find out.

Unwittingly, I, as a protégé of his sworn enemy, had invaded Draper's minor university fortress and he was determined to sort me out at dinner and bridge that very evening before I knew what hit me. The proud, stubborn, ostracized, and irascible Draper had engaged two young emissaries from his own moribund camp to invite me that afternoon to share the evening of my meticulous dissection. His scouring cross-examination of my background was as exhaustive and exhausting as I later discovered his Shakespearean research to be. I was grateful that Ross had earlier clued me in on departmental infighting. Draper was determined to sound out my scholarly quality that very same night and Prince Hamlet was the crux of the matter. Turf invasion is always dangerous.

Alas, I had something major to hide on *Hamlet* and whether Draper knew the specifics or not—which I doubt, even now—his maneuvers to find it out failed during an inquisition-like dinner conversation and Shakespeare-punctuated bridge that ended in total collapse and bad feeling for all of us at 1 a.m. My initiation into the intricacies of higher education had not let up since I got off the plane. His aggressive hostility had turned me off from the outset. I was determined not to spill any beans. He was equally determined to hold me hostage until he found out something substantive. We ended up with a standoff. Even though I had come from the enemy camp, I was really no threat on any count. In retrospect, he must have reached the conclusion that I was not a very penetrating scholar. During the rest of my tenure, we were civil, but never again engaged in anything more than perfunctory exchanges. We were not threats to one another.

In 1954, Draper was, and still remains posthumously, the most prolific researcher on Shakespeare that has ever lived—albeit that many of his pieces dealt with petty details. Buried in this relative backwater, he was indeed both jealous of preserving his reputation and aware of his neglect by his fellow university colleagues throughout the Shakespearean world. Brawner, the mink-coat chair, might even have purposely upset him out of rivalry, by informing him that his new recruit was a fellow Shakespearean who had studied under Columbia's Oscar James Campbell, the dean of American Shakespearean scholars for more than a quarter century, and Draper's nemesis. For over a dozen years, Draper and Campbell had carried on an international war in prestigious journals to topple one another over a major substantive issue: the validity of Campbell's original sources on Shakespeare. Their controversy was well known in the field, but not yet to me, still an MA neophyte. Draper was ultimately vindicated. But, at the time, I, like Rosencrantz and Guildenstern, had not the slightest idea of this dynamic tension framed as between meticulous and summary research. I had become, through an act of blind fate, placed in the middle of this conflict.

I was convinced, in February 1954, that Draper had not seen the draft or its original presentation in my master's essay, or the draft I sent to the *Quarterly*. Draper in his lifetime and the otherwise occupied Shakespearean world were denied these pregnant, but unpolished, findings until my 1992 lecture on quintessence in *Hamlet*, presented in London to the Society for the History of Alchemy and Chemistry, over forty years later.

If the truth be known then, as it will now be, when I arrived at WVU in 1954, I was carrying the long-sought-after mother lode of *Hamlet* studies. It was a prize that Draper would have given his soul to possess. I had casually picked it up crossing Division Avenue in Brooklyn as a child. But I had put it down again for forty years as I had been floating on a constantly moving carpet between earning my bread at business activity and the learned world. The aged Campbell at Columbia, who had had to endure countless *Hamlet* studies and conjectures during his quarter-century tenure, knew about the massiveness of my achievement back then and told me so. It was off the chart and beyond what any Shakespearean critics, then or now, knew about. I myself suspected that I had had the kind of once-in-a-half millennium breakthrough with Shakespeare that I later enjoyed in 1992 and 2006 with my equally startling discoveries about the ignored seventeenth-century foundations of Jonathan Swift's satire against John Locke and his disciples.

But in 1954, my stunning find of Polonius's wise saws, still unexploited elsewhere to this day, needed grounding in massive assimilation of a still-to-come, far more comprehensively focused Shakespearean research. We now have sources and research tools not available to Campbell, Draper and me earlier in the last century. Leaving my eleven-year post as a consultant for AT&T following its breakup in 1982, I returned to scholarly work to complete my book on Jonathan Swift, which required ten years of unrelenting research. The first edition, published in February 1992 on my seventieth birthday, received 28 positive reviews in journals representing 7 disciplines. As one reviewer said, my playful, sad, humane book demanded serious attention. I knew that Shakespeare still needed far more full-time years. Research on *Hamlet* alone, like wading through millions of sites on the Internet, could require a lifetime. But, like both my book on Swift and Locke, and my revelations on Laurence Sterne and Tolstoy's *War and Peace*, still on hold, the startling *Hamlet* discovery remained on my luckily long life's always teeming agenda.

Only now can I finally put the superstructure around that four-century missing evidence that will make *Hamlet* as transparent to any leading actor or public audience today as it was patently recognizable as daily experience to the far more *au courant* Elizabethan audience then. Fortunately, in 1954 at WVU, I arrived on the scene with merely apprentice credentials in the Shakespearean guild. If I had revealed or displayed anything more, a slippery sleuth and master craftsman like Draper would have run off with my booty.

CHAPTER SEVEN

1992 GLOBE LEGEND

When I returned forty years later in 1992 to my 1953 discovery of Paul as a source for *Hamlet*, I had to assimilate the massive amounts of new material written since my teaching in 1973 and establish a new trusted relationship with the then reigning authority on Shakespeare, the 1992 dean of Campbell's stature. In any field as vast as Shakespearean studies, only a handful among several thousand in each generation are hardwired to rise to preeminence.

Oscar James Campbell, the leading authority for decades before he was my early graduate advisor through 1954, had conferred his approval on me for my groundbreaking detective work on Polonius in *Hamlet*. But it wasn't until 1992, when I had returned full time to complete that original detective work, that I bonded with the eminent Andrew Gurr, Campbell's recognized Shakespearean equal in the decades before we met. Professor Gurr, Director of the Renaissance Texts Research Centre, served as a prime mover in the authentic restoration of Shakespeare's Globe Theater in Southwark, London. He provided me with an irreplaceable measure of caution and direction on the draft of my 1992 London lecture on quintessence in *Hamlet*. Gurr had meticulously reconstructed the minutest physical properties and matériel of Shakespeare's Globe Theater just as I was reconstructing the precise contemporary events, values, and sources of the play *Hamlet*. In addition, connecting the play with my own life here and now only adds new parallels to the credibility of my contemporary reconstruction of that Elizabethan ethos and the theme of my book. Gurr and I continued our new critical relationship and in November 2000, I was able to make some restitution for this patently uneven exchange.

Like Campbell, Gurr knew that I had made a very important original contribution that I was diligently completing in depth at Oxford's Bodleian Library. But establishing the authenticity of my 1953 key beyond a doubt depended on linking this masterpiece, as Shakespeare did, to the blockbuster contemporary leaders and issues on everyone's tongue in the stalls and pit on the occasion of its original performance in 1600. Audience recognition of allusions to contemporary figures provides alluring frames of reference. Shakespeare was not writing specifically for us. I needed a new scholarly discovery in 2000 of the drama's contemporary framework to underpin my own original discovery of its spiritual source in 1953.

Magic happened. Complementing my own earlier detective work and luck, I unearthed a buried, 1925 article in a Welsh journal, unlisted at Oxford's Bodleian Library or anywhere. With this new contemporary evidence, Gurr wrote me on 27 November 2000 that the 1925 article reached a "sane and cautious" conclusion that substantiated my own *Hamlet* breakthrough on source and would lead me to closure. It was a necessary piece in the St. Paul puzzle: namely, that the character of Hamlet merges contemporary facts about both the Earl of Essex and King James I, two critical figures, the first a key player and the other an aspirant, in determining the succession to the fading Elizabeth. They were two recognized humanists with great capacities for executive political power, like Hamlet, whose values were being marginalized in a material New World increasingly dominated by fortune hunters like Lord Burghley, the model for Polonius, and his son Robert Cecil, scornful of ethical values and humanistic concerns.

My detective work was compounded with ironies and extraordinary good luck that Gurr and I savored in our meetings at the Globe. Lilian Winstanley, an obscure, unheard-of scholar, had written a 1921 book brimming with her own excitement, *Hamlet and the Scottish Succession,* (Cambridge, 1921). Once the thrill of discovery subsided, she supplemented her brilliant findings by increasingly qualifying 1924 and 1925 articles documenting Shakespeare's heavy use of contemporary luminaries to provide substance to the burning issues of the day in the play *Hamlet*. It was one of those instances where initial enthusiasm based on personal hunches ultimately came under the control of later verifiable evidence. In Gurr's and my view, her buried 1925 article finally got it right, but this balanced record of still neglected convincing proofs had never appeared in any accessible bibliography or the foreground of Shakespearean studies. She was published in a now defunct regional journal. Shakespearean studies demand the highest national levels of scrutiny and credibility. Here, I had found buried gold away from the scholarly hub, unearthed 84 years before Shapiro.

Truth is known to be buried in a well. Winstanley's buried findings corroborated mine. But, if I hadn't found hers through a series of lucky hits, her great analysis would probably have been buried forever. I had first read Winstanley's original 1921 book, and had later stumbled by pure chance on an obscure bibliographic mention at the Bodleian Library of her 1924 article, only available in Wales. I, therefore, asked Gareth Jones, my esteemed Russian studies colleague and dear Welsh friend, to search out that 1924 article in the defunct *Aberystwyth Studies* 6:47–64. Any other scholar but my friend would have copied the 1924 article for me and let it go at that. But Gareth's dogged initiative and meticulous scholarship discovered the unrecorded existence of her reconsidered, final 1925 appraisal—her buried, more restrained, but convincing gem, in the later annual issue 7:37–50. Gurr and I concluded that after four years she had finally got it right, even though her insights continued lost from sight of the Shakespearean community. Score this major illumination on *Hamlet* up to the relentless scholarly discipline of the Welsh in 1925 and again in 2000. The mills of the gods grind slow, but exceeding fine.

My research since 1992 on the contemporary issues in *Hamlet*, the keystone of Paul in the character and plot, Shakespeare's own spiritual causes, and the relation of my own life to the play complete this book. These new discoveries, building on my earlier ones, have been greatly facilitated by Shapiro's 2005 edition of Shakespeare's 1599 life. He has been invaluable on the role of the Earl of Essex in the casting of the play, consistent with waning chivalry in 1599 and the search for Shakespeare's inspiration for the soliloquies.

Going beyond my own 2000 research on Essex, Shapiro finds Essex barging into Queen Elizabeth's bedroom before she is dressed on September 29, 1599 as a possible act of sedition, the last gasp of chivalry, and possible yoking with the closet scene wherein Hamlet barges in on his mother. While I am extremely grateful to Shapiro for adding brilliant confirming perspectives to my own earlier 2000 research on the centrality of the conflict between Essex and the adversarial Cecils at the core of the play, nonetheless, it is now my turn for closure.

There is a double delay here in the full illumination of the play *Hamlet* and of my own critical life decisions. Both emanate from the same currently undervalued aesthetic, spiritual, and European historical sources. As Hamlet—and I—finally recognized after his own fatal, delaying tactics, "There's a divinity that shapes our ends, / Rough-hew them how we will" (5.2.10–11). As for the second delay, it is only now and here, in this new century and this book, that I can at last simultaneously link my full findings with the benefit of a half-century of new scholarship and the history of the meaning of my own lifetime of crossing Division Avenues throughout New York's corporate and learned worlds. I have had my own half-century of fiddling and delay. It is here and now that I introduce executive allusions with the Bard's universal perspective that makes this classical drama apply for all time. Any performer, scholar, or audience connected with *Hamlet* will now be able to see the play in this long-delayed new light. As a corollary, readers will soon understand the basis of its riveting influence on my life. Neither Shakespeare nor I dare separate the universal values and the contemporary leadership history of the time. Each insight, source, and age buttresses the other.

Obviously Shakespeare's characters are composites of tales, histories, dramas, and contemporaries compressed and assimilated by his supreme imagination. Thanks to Winstanley, my unearthed source on Essex, and Shapiro, we can at last safely say that the protagonist of the play *Hamlet* is a composite of one mythic and two real contemporary figures: Amleth, originally from the twelfth-century Icelandic saga; contemporaneously, Robert Devereux, the Second Earl of Essex; and, James I. Amleth had gone through changes from Saxo Grammaticus across the centuries culminating in the so-called *Ur Hamlet* Elizabethan play, a then well-known, but now lost, 1590 forerunner. Next, Essex was Elizabeth's court favorite, sometime lover, and the last hope for those other conspiring lords, the army, and the populace who would depose her. Alongside Essex, they would all dump the father and son Lord Burghley-Sir Robert Cecil power dynasty around her. The other contemporary figure, the future absolutist James I, then James VI of Scotland, proved a less critical model for Hamlet.

At the risk of opening new controversy, I would add a fourth composite—that of Shakespeare's own psyche. As a London theatrical "player" and insider intimately familiar with the blow-by-blow dynastic stakes, Shakespeare was keenly aware of the late great Burghley (his model for Polonius) as master of statecraft and revels, who was thus a thorn in his side until Burghley's death in 1598.

Let's set this scene as personally experienced through Shakespeare's own heart and professional eyes. The play *Hamlet*, worked on in 1599, first appeared in the winter of 1600, before the beheading of Essex in February 1601. Queen Elizabeth was still making up her mind about succession and the beheading of Essex for treason. The play is thus both the gloomy harbinger and dramatic commentary on events leading up to the ax falling. The contemporary figures implicated in the unfolding of both this high climactic drama in the waning reign of Elizabeth and in the play itself are, as we have seen, Essex, the late Lord Burghley, his son Robert Cecil, the future James I, and quite unexpectedly, Shakespeare himself. Between them, the Cecils, father and son, were a dynasty in their own right, having been the chief counselors to all three Tudor heirs of Henry VIII and pending for James I, first of the Stuarts.

The 1925 Winstanley article makes us realize what visible major power struggle Shakespeare and his contemporaries were witnessing involving the intriguing Cecils, the suspicious Queen, and the prime mover Essex. Let her set the 1599 national scene that the play embodies.

> The Elizabethan age, so glorious in its prime, was ending when *Hamlet* was written in disillusion, in division of mind, and in profound melancholy; it ended also with the destruction of the Irish nationality, and it is this picture of profound and tragic gloom which, I believe, Shakespeare has transmitted for us into the pages of *Hamlet* (Winstanley, 50).

When the play first appeared, Essex and Shakespeare's patron, the Earl of Southampton, close friends, were suspected of sedition and both would soon sit in the Tower of London as traitors, having been found guilty of treason in a botched conspiracy to depose Elizabeth. Shakespeare's company came dangerously close to suffering her wrath in supporting them. Essex's downfall had been personally orchestrated by the late Burghley's son Robert Cecil.

According to Winstanley, like Hamlet, Essex had a deep love for his father, preferred his studies at Cambridge and the quiet life to the intrigue of the polluted court life mega-managed by the Cecils. In 1584, his urbanity and courtesy won over the hearts of the Queen and the people enhanced with this chivalric triumph as the head of the army at Cadiz in 1588. Like his father, he was leader in the Puritan religion. Sent by the Queen in 1599 to quell Irish rebellion, he, like his father before him, instead made common cause with the rebel leader Tyrone and demonstrated great generosity, sympathy, and deep affection in supporting Irish nationality. His enemy, Robert Cecil took advantage of Essex's absence to set the Queen against him for treason.

The death of Irish nationality occurred when a second general was sent to repudiate the terms of Essex. According to Winstanley, Shakespeare symbolizes the death of Irish nationality in Ophelia, the true love of Hamlet-Essex. Ophelia could only stand for Offaly or Kings County where Ireland and Essex met their fate. The rebels suffered their muddy death in watery bogs singing melancholy songs and laden with grassy garlands reminescent of Ophelia's own watery death.

While Shakespeare transfers the somber melancholy mood in England to *Hamlet* using Essex's and Ireland's fatal decline from 1599 to 1601, he is also linking the play with larger universal issues contributing to that nation's melancholy. The chivalric tradition characterized by honor, which Essex belatedly represents in its dying phases has already been satirized by Shakespeare's contemporary Cervantes's *Don Quixote*. Nonetheless,

Essex-Hamlet represent chivalry's positive replacement with the burgeoning Puritan Pauline tradition of "love thy neighbor."

With the ascendency of James I in 1603, England becomes Great Britain with new Puritan governmental powers and colonial policies that pit "love thy neighbor" against "exploit thy neighbor"—an unsolvable Puritan dilemma. The destruction of Irish nationality at the end of Elizabeth's reign with the personal orchestration of the Cecils anticipate the Puritan dilemma in the New World where sacrificial religious freedom conflicts with lucrative commercial enterprise. Throughout the seventeenth century, this conflict played out in the more distant colonies until the semblance of Puritan love became a cover for Puritan commerce. Shakespeare's melancholy reflects the rise of the Cecils and their self-serving individualism; their leadership enterprise justified slavery at the beginning of this global systemic change. My own experience growing up in a Puritan household with careers in both the corporate and learned worlds merely reinforced my own gloom in the further cumulative decline of ethical values.

It is this melancholy mood created by the leadership shift in priorities from virtue to vice in the highest places of executive power. Fortune as strumpet or greedy prostitution exploited the New World brimming with human and natural resources. The commercial opportunities led to permanent imbalances in wealth and power. Irresponsible leadership in the ascendancy is the play *Hamlet's* most recurring key satirical theme. Thus the dramatic tension in the play is between satire and deserved demise of all vicious fortune hunters. Meanwhile, the tragedy centers on the lonely soul searcher Hamlet who goes in the opposite direction of self-evaluation and virtue. He concludes that whatever schemers contrive, final revolution of fickle Fortune's wheel is certain death for all players; thus in the end none can circumvent God's will. That is the play's somber resolution of all those graveside and stage corpses that pile up for the usual generational cast changes in Act 5, just as in real life. Until now, modern audiences have viewed *Hamlet* without knowing that Shakespeare has embedded within the play one set of ethics for soul seekers and a more insensitive credo for bargain hunters.

Primarily, St. Paul's New Testament credo creates that essential tension and the play's wheel spinning rotation between exploiting or loving thy neighbor. Paul's Christian credo compels the dialectic of the soul in rational soliloquies to move from acts of individual feeling to communal acts based on access to divine intervention and grace. As a satiric counterpoint, Shakespeare has also introduced a parody of Paul's credo with humorous self-serving laws for fortune seekers blind to the self-sacrificial acts God demands of the soul. The diametrical objectives of the two credos, self-aggrandizing or self-sacrifice, exploitation or love, dominate the entire action throughout and reveal the vast distances for Elizabethan audiences between the ideas of fickle Fortune and heaven-directed divine grace, body and soul, evil and good; the fierce opposites in the endless conflicts of human destiny.

CHAPTER EIGHT

RULE BY PRAGMATIC FORTUNE

Winstanley's long buried detective work, Shapiro's recent research, and my insights dramatically dovetail and mutually confirm each other. Burghley is the worldly contemporary Shakespeare draws on for the old father, Polonius, in the play, the fortune-seeking icon. The character Polonius rings all the changes on Lord Burghley's life as the vain, foolish, and villainous counselor. As they are carbon copies, they think pragmatically. Will a scheme work regardless of any ethical or other ill consequences? Thus, contrasting sacrificial Paul with fortune-seeking Burghley on their sets of ethical principles seems just right. Spiritual values expressed in the Pauline soliloquies challenge the material practicality in Polonius-Burghley wise saws.

Shapiro misses the adversarial struggle between Paul and Polonius. Although Shapiro credits Montaigne's 1580 essays as slowly being imported from France as providing possible sources for Hamlet's soliloquies, my parallel discovery is that melancholy Paul, an Elizabethan staple, has even greater ethical and psychological significance for Hamlet's reflection and consciousness throughout the play, and for development of the new salvation theme throughout the innovative Christian revenge plot first introduced in the revised Act 4.

The issue is executive leadership. Paul's invocation for stark sacrifice as preparation reduces Burghley's practices to artifice. The specter of death hangs over the real events and the play of *Hamlet* like a pall for Shakespeare himself and all Elizabethans. There was a dearth of leadership—as now—to heed Paul's universal rallying cry for fundamental human sacrifice and removal from worldliness by rational renewing of the mind that undergirds his pivotal credo in Romans 12–13.

> And be not ye fashioned lyke unto this World: *but* be ye changed in your shape, by the renuying of your mynde, that ye maye prove What is the good, and acceptable, and perfect Wyl of God" (Rom. 12:1–2, emphasis added).

That ethical credo illuminates the play with an Elizabethan thrust that future performers and New World audiences sorely miss. The same credo is mine too. It is the most important virtuous use of Paul in the play. The humanistic renewing of the mind through the soliloquies in *Hamlet*, the principles in Romans 12–13, and my life all progress from melancholy world-weariness and angst, to the agency of providential design and inner peace.

While the incongruity of American education persists in advocating the self-aggrandizing advice of the bumbling fool and secretive knave Polonius, Elizabethans could recognize his real life model, Lord Burghley. Generations of American high school seniors over the last century have been forced to memorize his treacherous, main-chance maxims nationwide as American fortune-seeking gospel. I have seen these worldly maxims inscribed in corporate board rooms, and, more often than not, in the calculating hearts of the upward-bound as the touchstone of self-interested executive power and fortune. This ironic misreading and disconnect by a whole nation led astray by pragmatic fortune, while neglecting the communal soul, would have led Elizabethans to question the sanity, integrity, and degradation of American public education and its future consequences.

Burghley and the character Polonius are mirror images. Burghley's biographer, Martin Hume in *The Great Lord Burghley* (Longmans, Green, 1898), without alluding to Polonius, nonetheless, describes Burghley's maxims to his son, at length, that bear a remarkable likeness to Polonius's. For example: "He that payeth another man's debts seeketh his own decay;" "With thine equals [be] familiar yet respectful;" "Trust not any man with thy life, credit, or estate" (25–26). Hume sums up Burghley's proverbs by saying, "his was a selfish and ungenerous gospel, but a prudent and circumspect one" (26). If you want good fortune with only the façade of virtue, these rules worked at the pinnacle of three Tudor reigns for Burghley. They are very sound indeed for all businessmen in today's highly competitive global market. A pure façade hiding selfish behavior is all one needs. They provide a formula for the current global economic, ethical, and psychic meltdown.

While preparing this memoir, I discovered the second satirical use of the four connected satirical uses Shakespeare makes of Romans 12–13; the ethical heart of the play. In the play narrative, as in the Elizabethan court and even now, good fortune and vicious, immature behavior win. Youthful dalliance and the reliving of it dominate the play. Laertes has gone off to Paris for a hedonistic good time, not for spiritual improvement, so his father Polonius believes. The old fool sends Reynaldo to spy on him. In real life, Burghley had done the same with his own wastrel son in Paris to no avail. In this scene, Polonius, the *voyeur extraordinaire*, requires Reynaldo to impugn his son's character as a libertine in the Parisian fleshpots: "Dishonor him" (2.1.28). Checking among Laertes's acquaintances, the emissary should imply "wanton, wild, and usual slips" including "gaming...drinking, fencing, swearing / Quarreling, drabbing" (2.1.22–27), that is, entering "a brothel" (2.1.63). He is also to be framed as having "a savageness in unreclaimèd blood" (2.1.35) and "of general assault" (2.1.36).

Once again, as this detective found out, the playwright has dipped into the recognizable chapters from Romans that define Christian ethics for all time. In ascribing vicious behavior to his son, Polonius has simply repeated all of Paul's catalog of vices from Romans 13. "Let us walke honestly, as in the day, not in ryotyng and drunkenesse, neyther in chamerying and wantonesse, neyther in stryfe and envying. But put ye on the Lorde Jesus Christe, and make no provision for the fleash, to fulfyl the lustes thereof" (Rom. 13:13–14). If in the play, Shakespeare has relied on Paul's Christian virtues as the necessary requirements of royal succession for his contemporaries and his royal Dane Hamlet, would they not serve a presidential aspirant in our comparable time or even a broker of systemic change?

The value judgments that Elizabethans made in distinguishing the motivations of Hamlet and Polonius need to be viewed within the contemporary issues of the struggle for governmental power and succession at the end of Elizabeth's reign. This play about illegitimate succession and its corrupt supporters responds one-on-one to this hot issue at the time. Modern audiences need these historical facts to understand how the profound 'fell opposites' (5.2.61–62) of good and evil resonate at the core of Shakespeare's vision. To run away from history leads away from the essential keys to the artist's value and values, as is transparently evident here. As we will now see, Shakespeare took sides and had a propaganda role to play in these contemporary events.

Shakespeare has multiple uses for the all-too-familiar life and lifestyle of Burghley, England's prime court figure, as the character Polonius. On the Elizabethan Richter scale, no figure registered more power and wealth and provoked more fear and hatred for half a century in England than William Cecil, Lord Burghley. In many ways, the three Tudor regimes after Henry VIII, ending with Elizabeth in 1603, had exhausted Elizabethan society through wars, extravagances, and taxes. These, Burghley had loyally supervised officially as Minister of State and unofficially as Master of Intrigue and Master of Revels for their succeeding royal highnesses. Polonius fulfills these same roles of intrigue and revels for the vicious usurper Claudius.

There was an adversarial relationship between Hamlet and Polonius. Similarly, Essex and Burghley were engaged in a parallel conflict. Ultimately, Robert Cecil, Burghley's son and successor, challenged Essex to a keen power struggle leading to the death of Essex in the later years of Elizabeth's reign.

Because Burghley had the kind of consummate imperial power that Polonius can only flail at, he was also the most hated by the powerful noblemen Essex, Elizabeth's favorite, and Southampton, Shakespeare's patron. These courtiers had known Burghley only too well, as they had both been brought up as children in Burghley's home under his legal protection and surveillance. In their adult lives, these two remained very close associates. Essex became ironically, while an intimate in the bedroom to Elizabeth, the vain hope of the populace seeking relief from her and Burghley's late monarchical tyranny.

What are the essential facts on the Essex conspiracy to dethrone Elizabeth familiar to Shakespeare's audience when he is composing and staging *Hamlet*? The childless Elizabeth in her sixties still refuses at any point to name an heir. James VI of Scotland, who will become her successor as James I of Great Britain, has the most logical blood line through Mary, Queen of Scots. Essex, too, has an outside chance to succeed her. As a master stroke, Burghley's son Robert Cecil intrigues to isolate her favorite by arranging for Essex to lead a large army to quell rebellion in Ireland. Winstanley has shown us, once in Ireland, Essex, generously and impulsively, knights scores of loyal noblemen; he then makes common cause with the rebel Irish demands for freedom from English tyranny, as his noble father had before him during a similar invasion.

While Essex is pinned down in Ireland, Cecil builds a case against him with the queen. Returning to England, isolated with lots to answer for to the impatient queen, Essex decides to lead his own populous rebellion against her tyranny, which Cecil nips in the bud. One Sunday morning, Cecil personally leads Essex and Southampton to the Tower. On the previous day, Shakespeare's company had presented Richard II, the king who instigates his own deposition, as a scarcely-veiled, symbolic support for Essex. As for the future James I biding his time in Scotland, once he hears that Essex is in disgrace, he changes English horses in mid-stream, bidding his emissary negotiate his royal British future through Robert Cecil, who will become his ultimate friend and first minister in court.

Shapiro and the Welsh scholar Winstanley neatly establish the connection between contemporary and universal values in the play by identifying the similarities between Essex, James I, and the character of Hamlet. All three had mothers who married with indecent haste the murderers of their husbands. The father of Essex, noted for his chivalric honor, probity, and service, was poisoned by the powerful and licentious Earl of Leicester. All three are lonely, misunderstood scholars isolated in the midst of a court that intrigues against them; all three have passionate interests in philosophy and theology, with Hamlet wishing to return to Luther's Wittenberg University. They are isolated humanists with values akin to mine. The doomed Essex had a separate reputation as an Oxford Master of Arts, an outstanding poet with interests in plays and players, a distinguished military strategist with contempt for courtiers, a profound love for his noble father, and a winning charm and urbanity. Shakespeare, nonetheless, could still hold out hope for James I who could not arrive too soon for his public audience. Through Shakespeare's eyes, when *Hamlet* was first performed in 1600, the formerly glorious Elizabethan era was ending in disillusionment and profound sadness. Winstanley called it a time of collective melancholy. The humanist values, as now, were being buried by the pragmatic fortune hunters like Polonius, Claudius, and their hangers-on.

Those firmly entrenched in the real world of here and now cannot be bothered with these time-consuming nagging questions of human destiny. If worldly success measured by power and wealth instead of wisdom and virtue become the overriding criteria for a good life today, it would be difficult to find a finer exemplar in any age than Lord Burghley. That Shakespeare decided to attack him tangentially and posthumously in *Hamlet*, through the character of Polonius, suggests that he felt his contemporary role as playwright entitled him to weigh in on the key power relationship between the public theater and the state. The timing of the play in 1600, two years after Burghley's death and following Essex's aborted attempt to seize power, makes it news. This coup was abetted by Shakespeare's erstwhile patron Southampton, who also landed in the Tower, and Shakespeare's company, too, thwarted by Burghley's son and successor, just three years before Elizabeth's death.

These news events in the public domain can all be coupled with the enormous claims that Shakespeare makes in this particular play itself for the pivotal role of the theater in influencing society. The structure of the play means to separate Paul's Christian ethics, a hard road to follow, from Polonius's garbled version of the wise saws, and here, senile wantonness, which together describe his dependence on fortune. Hamlet sums up the old man's lechery. "He's for a jig or a tale of bawdry, or he sleeps" (2.2.500–501). Shakespeare ties together Fortune with wantonness by personifying this abstraction. "Out, out, thou strumpet Fortune! All you gods / In general synod take away her power!" (2.2.493–94). But Fortune wins the day over classical ideals and Christian ethics, the foundation stones of humanism, by the end of the play and the beginning of the modern era of inventions and discoveries.

And Fortune's winner is the character Fortinbras; Shakespeare's clever pun on "strong in arms," referring to the interchangeability of strength and power. His ambitious shadow opens and closes the play. In Act 1, Scene 1, Horatio denigrates him as young, filled with pride, of unimproved mettle, hot and full, and sharked up with a list of lawless resolutions. He wishes to recover "by strong hand" (1.1.106) Danish lands. In Act 4, Scene 1, Hamlet contrasts the inactivity of his own humanism with the forced march of Fortinbras with "ambition puffed…Exposing what is mortal and unsure / To all that fortune, death, and danger dare" (4.4.50, 4.4.52–53). He sees Fortinbras causing the imminent death of 20,000 men fighting for a worthless plot of land, "an eggshell" (4.4.54). And yet it is Fortune and the ambitious Fortinbras who is left to pick up the pieces for well-motivated, but headstrong youth and corrupt absolute monarchy.

CHAPTER NINE

OUTRAGEOUS FORTUNE OR REDEMPTIVE LOVE

The strongest clue to the major theme in *Hamlet* appears most eloquently in the play within the play.

> Out, out, thou strumpet Fortune! All you gods
> In general synod take away her power!
> Break all the spokes and fellies from her wheel,
> And bowl the round nave down the hill of heaven
> As low as to the fiends! (2.2.493–497)

With these lines on the Wheel of Fortune, Shakespeare enters into a direct conversation on this critical image with the great writers who have come before him going back to Tibetan Buddhism, pagan Rome, the classical Christian Boethius, Chaucer, Dante, and Machiavelli among others.

These lines are anticipated by the sexual wit combat on the strumpet Fortune between Hamlet, Rosencrantz, and Guildenstern in the same scene.

> Hamlet: Then you live about her [Fortune's] waist, or in the middle of her favors?
> Guildenstern: Faith, her privates we.
> Hamlet: In the secret parts of Fortune? Oh, most true, she is a strumpet. (2.2.232–236)

The epitome on the two mentions of the strumpet Fortune leads inevitably to the greatest compliment Shakespeare ever extended to his own craft of classical drama. Hamlet, speaking to Polonius says,

> Do you hear, let them be well used, for they are the abstract and brief chronicles of the time. After your death you were better have a bad epitaph than their ill report while you live. (2.2.523–526)

Our present day's own ill report begins with the 30 Years War at the time of Shakespeare's death in 1616. The same bad news continues even until now, almost 400 years later, when the global neighborhood fights to humanity's death over nuclear dominance. Institutions and individuals with universal accord have chosen fortune over the human soul, which leads inexorably to exploiting and beggaring rather than loving thy neighbor. The learning curve can only be devoted to one of these options in a single lifetime. Only once more in the gravediggers scene, which records Fortune's sure triumphs of death for everyone, does Shakespeare again mention her catastrophic wheel.

> Hamlet: Why, e'en so, and now my Lady Worm's, chapless [no lower jaw], and knocked about the mazard [head] with a sexton's spade. Here's fine revolution [turn of Fortune's wheel], an we had the trick to see't. Did these bones cost no more the breeding but to play at loggets [bowling pins] with them? Mine ache to think on't. (5.1.88–93)

Something is rotten in Denmark and, likewise, in the modern New World when all classes are seduced by the opportunities falsely presented by the strumpet Fortune. She offers ignominious death by transfixing an entire modern culture in the democratic prospect of societal success at the expense of others. The losers are the community at large. Also lost are the opportunities for redeeming the individual soul by loving thy neighbor.

The Wheel of Fortune, *Rota Fortunae,* ultimately resembles the bhavacakra wheel of becoming, depicted throughout ancient Indian art and literature. It was picked up by Cicero and then given a Christian interpretation by Boethius (d. 524). In medieval literature, the wheel featured death of the mighty as in the gravediggers scene. Chaucer's "Monk's Tale," from *The Canterbury Tales*, reveals the fall from power and happiness to sorrow and death. The 13th-century poem *Carmina Burana* gives the wheel a bad name featuring rising to the highest power as the condition for fate's wheel to roll you to your nadir. Dante, Machiavelli, Lydgate, and the Arthurian romances used the concept of the wheel as an instructive of the treacherousness of fate, all easily available to Shakespeare. Shakespeare also used the wheel in *King Lear, Macbeth*, and *Henry V*.

The play *Hamlet* is about the absolute power of the dramatist and the relative power of the 'fell opposites' (5.2.61–62), that is, the mighty opposition between universal good and evil, virtue and vice, soul and body, as they play out daily in every human heart and hearth on earth. When we move to these larger issues of classical tragedy, *Hamlet* is about nothing if not the fateful choosing of sides, both in the play and in real life, by both the characters and the audience at that point in time. If you are the best available humanist, and you know it, like Shakespeare, sooner or later, you are going to weigh the options on these forces and counterforces and put each of them out there in their most exquisite form. Every moment we have choices. Tragedy in drama may scare you; you may even go down on your knees like Claudius, but it is not ordering you to do anything. Unlike authority figures telling you what to do next, dramatic tragedy gives you an accurate picture of available options in your own autonomy. It may not be much, but at least it's in focus.

How do we choose? Both Paul and Shakespeare agree on the dialectic of the soul as the most important command of what God requires of all humans. Paul at the opening of Romans 12 lists as God's first command the "renewing of the mind."

Paul's sacrificial way through this dialectic of the soul is the larger message in these three final chapters and represents my most important discovery achieved in writing this book. Once again:

> geve up your bodyes a quicke sacrifice, holy, acceptable unto God, which is your reasonable service. And be not ye fashioned lyke unto this World: *but* be ye changed in your shape, by the renuying of your mynde, that ye maye prove What is the good, and acceptable, and perfect Wyl of God" (Rom. 12:1–2, emphasis added).

Hamlet offers his own pithy summary of what Paul calls "renewing of the mind," and I call "dialectic of the soul," which Hamlet calls "large discourse:"

> Sure he that made us with such large discourse,
> Looking before and after, gave us not
> That capability and godlike reason
> To fust [grow moldy] in us unused. (4.4.37–40)

This passage confirms my profound Pauline discovery. Paul's two chapters beginning with God's command of renewing the mind, are the ethical foundation stone of all of his epistles, the play, and my own non-conforming lifestyle. The actions of all the characters in the play and in his audience can be easily calibrated along a continuum extending from the extreme, rare, sacrificial life demanding daily self-evaluation, to the other extreme daily commonplace of Fortune's slave.

Shapiro in his 2005 book on the metaphors of the play has not seen the Pauline connection, but he has discovered that in his second revision of the unwieldy script, Shakespeare removed honor as the major obsession of heroic action. Shapiro's contribution provides full credence to the Pauline influence. In Act 4, Shakespeare removed a critical soliloquy on Fortinbras, honor, and consciousness to re-orient the traditional revenge tragedy plot to a divine prerogative, inviting damnation for inaction or salvation for removing the cancer in Denmark through dialectic of the soul.

Once Hamlet realizes that he is the agent of a divine hand, "heaven ordinant" (5.2.48), and not a victim of outrageous fortune, personal stress and self-obligation cease. Hamlet is almost giddy in making riotous humor over Polonius's dead body and mocking the carnival of death with the clownish gravediggers. That he has followed the Pauline injunction to work out the will of God for himself may be summarized in his final convictions that from the providential standpoint "the readiness is all" (5.2.220) and in his belated acknowledgment that "There's a divinity that shapes our ends, / Rough-hew them how we will" (5.2.10–11). Translated: I got nowhere on my own, but then there is a consummate architect that determines our destinies accessible for us in the vast public domain of the communal soul, if we will work them out.

But of all the forces and counterforces on this pivot in European time, none seems more pivotal than whether we live in and under a providential creation, that is, under an overarching omnipotent, monotheistic god, or whether each and every one of us must go it alone in governance and daily life. Is there a divine skyhook like those monotheistic religions say? Or is there a natural skyhook, as Plato said, where each of us, as a microcosm, is a piece that fits into the communal macrocosm? The first two questions ask, are we agents of well-ordered divine or natural forces? Or, finally, is there no skyhook, no God, so that we're all left to our own devices and private laws? In which case, it's meaningless to cry out, God or Mother Nature help us!

The play *Hamlet* concentrates on the audience's constant, unequal struggle between evil and good universally. The play dramatizes the decisions of average characters on the fence between good and evil, who should discern better. Polonius obviously feeds the more powerful seductive side, making evil pass for good. The American psyche has that down pat. For those with more abundance than others, pleasurable "liberty and the pursuit of happiness" beats attending to a painful conscience or looking in the mirror. Yet, true to all human nature, the choice of good and evil is forever open to characters and audience. In contrast, Hamlet is constantly asking the universal audience and human betrayers, like Rosencrantz and Guildenstern, his mother, and Ophelia, to come clean on the basis of friendship and love. At the very least, love thy neighbor takes the more seductive choice of evil out of the equation. The play is credible evidence of the implications of choice, not prescription.

While 1992 and 2000 became new milestones in my *Hamlet* breakthroughs, all my life prepared me for this coordinated series of revelations. The ethos I developed when young, so different from my father's and my contemporaries, coincides with the world Shakespeare inhabited. From childhood, I had adopted a non-conformist philosophy, rather than a religion, out of Romans 12:2 that would keep me from committing myself to institutions, fashions, and received opinion generally. In the 1930s, I had voted thumbs down on Polonius's wise saws in high school, but that was only one incident in thousands.

Fortune in America on Polonius's terms seemed no more than a lottery, with all international neighbors competing with us or envying us or hating us. Along the way, concerned aunts and uncles, peers, and teachers chided me in that I wasn't joining the way of the world. I lived this isolating way of life that also harbored distressing psychological components, ultimately requiring about nine years to be thoroughly worked through in therapy during the 1960s when I was in my forties. Touchingly, when I reached adulthood, my brother John, who had been on my case all along, as a last resort, bought me a stylish fedora hat, which I promptly left under a chair at an Automat restaurant, and a pipe and a packet of tobacco, which rotted in a desk drawer. Is it any wonder that when I finally studied *Hamlet* at Columbia in 1949 at 27 years of age, Shakespeare and the character Hamlet became old friends soon after becoming new acquaintances?

There are two providential, humanistic agents in the play *Hamlet*: Hamlet and Shakespeare. The dramatist has Hamlet assume madness, suffer Pauline melancholy, expose time-serving followers around Claudius, as well as Ophelia's unexamined obedience to her father and, now and then, speak soliloquies to himself and us. After a long while, the playwright decides to have him murder Polonius and turn that action into a portent that he has become God's surrogate, the sacrificial agent of divine justice, in accordance with Romans 13. In the remaining acts, Shakespeare has him selectively quote the Bible for the first time in the play, referencing Matthew 10:29: "There is special providence in the fall of a sparrow" (5.2.217–18). These references reveal a new found equanimity as the now calm protagonist who predicts, offhandedly, that his mission will come when it will come. Shakespeare plays *deus ex machina* for the Christian God. All the while, the thoroughly involved audience, not so sure, is on the edge of its seats, waiting for Claudius's inevitable day of God's reckoning.

Good and evil are purposely unevenly matched in *Hamlet*, but the play rotates around the axis of which way human destiny will proceed. The dramatist gives the characters and his audience three choices. Three ways of living one's life impinge on each other in the play: classicism, Christianity, and fortune, as practiced from the fixed focus of each of the characters. Medieval traditions have been expunged. Only Hamlet and his dramatist appreciate the ironic interplay among classical ideals, Christianity, and fortune, and his soliloquies move among these readings of human destiny adroitly in the process of constructing a final direction in a transitional European era of systemic change. Fortune and vice, rather than virtues or belief systems, govern Claudius and the toadying crew around him. Shakespeare plays with this third option of human destiny: fortune, laying beyond classicism and Christianity, calling it blind chance, the luck of the draw. Never mind good and evil, Fortune is the big winner in *Hamlet*. Good fortune is the ring of pleasure as the evil king and his intimates enjoy the funeral meats. Bad fortune is combating evil under overwhelming odds. "The slings and arrows of outrageous fortune" (3.1.59) have knocked Hamlet's youth into a tizzy.

We are now done with fortune and the comic characters and the superficial American comedy as we move to tragedy, and the other options of human destiny, classical ideals, and Christianity. We also come to the climax of my humanist detective work, the book, and my life. Aristotle warned us that great tragedy can achieve the full catharsis of the emotions of pity and terror in us. The terror is that we may all be in harm's way for our own or our nation's wrong communal choices. Shakespeare achieves these emotions. Thus, in the twenty-first century, we move upwards to tragedy and the play's mystery. For when we leap from the detached comedy of individual fools and knaves to tragedy, the implications become communal and profound, no less so for implicating each individual in all audiences, past and future.

CHAPTER TEN

THE PAULINE HAMLET

In the play *Hamlet*, Shakespeare places all humans along a spectrum from "bestial oblivion" (4.4.41) to "large discourse" (4.4.37), that is renewing the mind. At the low end they merely sleep and feed. But, if one chooses the exploitive Wheel of Fortune over Paul's love thy neighbor, each of us from whatever time or place becomes the plaything of Fortune. Consequently, we become degraded to bestial oblivion. That is the Pauline exhortation exemplified in the gravedigger's scene and the corpses strewn out on stage in the final scene. Simply, we use the warlike tools agreed on by the *consensus gentium* for choosing Fortune, "passion's slave" (3.2.71). Behind whatever self-deluding façade are the debilitating seven deadly vices or sins: lust, gluttony, greed, sloth, wrath, envy, and pride. These excesses lead to terror, war, and death. Meanwhile, Paul's and Shakespeare's golden mean for living peacefully in a neighborhood depend on cultivating the seven community sustaining virtues: faith, hope, love, justice, fortitude, prudence, and temperance. They promote the golden mean of live and let live.

In addition to this monumental conclusion, Shakespeare has chosen four specific passages from Paul's Romans 12, 13. Why then does Shakespeare integrate them as the mysterious core in *Hamlet*? Shakespeare has no religious squeamishness about introducing this well-worn Christian advice of Paul through the parodying window of Polonius's wise saws early in Act 1, and again in Polonius's instructions to Reynaldo in Act 2. But these are the comic uses of Romans 12, 13 that I uncovered. The other two discoveries from the same source deal with the dialectic mystery of the tragedy and Paul's Christian revenge.

Hamlet represents the first attempt by a dramatist to add the Judaeo-Christian tradition to the steady Elizabethan diet of classical revenge tragedy. In breaking new ground, Shakespeare falls back on the Old Testament and New Testament as his source books. Hamlet compares Polonius, the biblical illiterate, to Jephthah in the Old Testament, whom God punishes for sacrificing his daughter for a battlefield gain. Paul is our Christian lawgiver here, and he sets down the new, Christian way of revenge. It is a far, far cry from classical revenge, which gets very personal and gruesome, even when the gods are afflicting each other or unfortunate mortals in their path. We have also come a long way from the Old Testament with God jealously guarding His own omnipotence and omnipresence. Classical gods were like that also. Ironically, Paul sets down his law of Christian revenge in that same thirteenth chapter of the Epistle to the Romans, the central juridical district for the then-known Western World. Specifically,

> For he [the prince] is ey minister of God for thy wealth. But if thou doo evyl, feare: for he beareth not the sworde in vayne; for he is the minister of GOD, revenger of Wrath on hym that dooth evyl (Rom. 13:4).

Fredson Bowers and others have noted Hamlet's recognition that the killing of Polonius sanctifies his divine role, but they did not pick up the Pauline justification, my fourth and final reference. The chapter also contains instructions on obedience to secular rulers who have swords, which picks up on Shapiro's analysis of the play as a new style revenge tragedy about salvation. Here is the New Testament authorization of the divine right of kings. It may come as a relief to learn that I am not alone in identifying the Romans source for Christian revenge. One other Shakespearean has seen the importance of Romans 13:1–4 as biblical authorization for Hamlet's revenge. At the same time, he has missed the recurring thread of this familiar biblical source on Pauline ethics in the play that I have located. Roland Mushat Frye in *The Renaissance Hamlet* (Princeton, 1984) has carefully spotted this key verse, Romans 13:4.

Hamlet suddenly realizes, when he impetuously kills Polonius behind the arras, that God's providence has been central to this event and has given him a sign that he is the true prince of Denmark. Hamlet is sophisticated enough to interpret the occasion of Polonius's death as the sign of providential intervention—the Ghost's messages didn't cut it. He understands in his shortest soliloquy that he is no longer going it alone and that he has become the living sacrifice of divine purposes: "But heaven hath pleased it so / To punish me with this, and this with me, / That I must be their scourge and minister" (3.4.180–182). Paraphrased, this killing indicates that I have a divine role to play. Providential intervention brings Hamlet to his fatal destiny as sacrificial agent, in this instance, as royal minister of God.

Shakespeare's and Hamlet's humanistic thought processes in the play—like those of the public audience—fluctuate among the classical and the separate Old and New Testament modes of revenge. Hamlet's understanding is that the climactic killing of Polonius falls within the New

Testament mode. Shakespeare hand delivers Romans 12–13 to Hamlet and his audience in Act 3.4 to convince all that divine authority superintended Polonius's death through his sacrificial agent, the foreordained minister of God.

The character of Hamlet suffered agonies of betrayal and his own inconclusive decision-making before reaching the Shakespearean humanistic accommodation between Pauline Christianity and Montaigne's modern skepticism. By contrast, neither Shakespeare nor I had any blockage in adapting the humanist compromise. The careful reading of humanistic texts, including Shakespeare, and my detective work on the critical importance of Romans 12 and 13 for Elizabethans, transformed me to search for a more profound *consensus gentium* on the human condition beyond extant shallow American value systems.

The lure of "outrageous fortune" (3.1.59) never got in my way. If I became in any way presidential, I never inclined toward public office because that route to executive power always seemed damnedly tied to bestial fortune as a first necessity. Although eminently qualified, my brother John, too, found this negative priority had stymied his election when he ran for Congress from Hawaii in 1976.

In his art and person, Shakespeare capitalized in his new revenge tragedy on what the original humanists Marsilio Ficino and Pico della Mirandola first attempted in the second half of the fifteenth century—to bring into harmony Christian theology with Platonic philosophy, the divine with the secular. Shakespeare defines his classical humanist position by presenting Hamlet as the epitome of the classical virtues, and through his famous passage on human potential, "What a piece of work is a man" (2.2.304–305) as both awesome and the humoral quintessence of dust. As a humanist, Shakespeare reconciles his classicism with Christianity by very specific allusions to Catholic doctrine and rituals. Claudius has vacated salvation in heaven for the good life here, but before the play ends, falls on his knees, too late to forestall divinely-ordered revenge. At that point, Hamlet does not kill him because in this penitent pose he would receive his free ticket to heaven thanks to Christ's sacrifice, which he did not deserve. Meanwhile, the Ghost of Hamlet's father functions solely in the punitive sphere which Paul only allows as providential Christian style revenge in Romans 13. Similarly, Hamlet eschews "not to be" (3.1.57) because he knows not what heaven has in store for suicides, although we get an inkling when poor Ophelia, a presumed suicide, has shortened burial rites in anticipation of her eternal damnation.

The play *Hamlet* and my life both center on humanism. One informs the other simultaneously, and never more so than in the humanistic originality of their major themes and denouements. My father unwittingly pushed me toward "godless" humanism, without realizing that this analytical philosophy could easily countenance love thy neighbor and the possibility of a divine force as essential facts of life. At the same time, my humanistic position would be liberated from the restrictive, elitist doctrine of predestination from which I had already been excluded by being, to my father, a prime suspect for the anti-Christ.

Humanist philosophers have raised questions about absolute and relative values, certainties and mysteries in every field from religion, governance, the arts, science, medicine, psychiatry, ethics, and daily life. The unfolding baroque era would have us all singing, playing, and dancing intricately, radiantly, and joyously in mysterious ensemble, while Hobbes, in that same era, would proclaim anathema on the entire species as certainly mean, nasty, and brutish. European monarchs including James I, and oligarchic adventurers including Shakespeare's fortune-oriented friends were already certainly vying to merchandise, colonize, and go to war over the Americas.

If anything, I have learned in writing this book that life's major choice is certainly between spiritual and worldly values. On one side, there is a sense of mission to identify wisdom and virtue represented in the saints, models, grandparents, parents, and siblings possessed of the peaceful virtues described as influences on my life. Wealth and power, epitomized by Shakespeare as fortune, is the riskier option.

Shakespeare puts today's audience on a pivot between current and these classical mores. On one hand, the tendency in our impatient era is to put all the blame on Hamlet for intellectualizing, fiddling, and diddling—particularly his Oedipal fixation with his mother's incestuous sheets, instead of getting on with the job, obvious to the audience, of avenging his father's murder by eliminating Claudius and the toadies around him. Similarly, I dawdled in graduate school until I was 45, at a time when wealth and power were comfortably within my grasp. But Hamlet is Shakespeare's agent, and the dramatist could have had Hamlet efficiently do his duty in the first act so that audiences for the last four hundred years could have caught transportation home before darkness set in around them.

On the other hand, classical tragedies of Sophocles and Euripides deal with the profound, darker, inexact issues in human life that resonate at the core of our being. A sigh outside the province of science may be our most poignant, strictly human expression because it comes unbidden from our deepest emotions, and when it appears, says so much to each of us in our aloneness. Like a sigh from our soul, tragedy brings us to our own life and death in all its starkness and does not leave us when the curtain is rung down. Our remaining life is the sixth act; our death, the seventh, and what we leave behind spiritually, the eighth. Shakespeare's eighth act is one of the greatest commentaries on what it is to be an engaged human instead of solely "a pipe for Fortune's finger / To sound what stop she please" (3.2.69–70).

CHAPTER ELEVEN

WAKING THE SOUL

If our age finds neglected stewardship of nature reaching a dangerous tipping point, Shakespeare believed leadership for determining the course of human nature similarly in crisis in 1600. The keystone of his argument in *Hamlet* is his imaginative contradictory destiny for the species, "quintessence of dust" drawn from learning and Genesis. Metaphorically, we are on the cusp of rising to the sublime or sinking back to primordial chaos. Based on the tendencies of his cast, individually and collectively, we show signs of moving in both directions.

This book has already developed the evidence for the heretofore ignored emphasis on the spiritual Pauline Hamlet, but in doing so bypassed the intertwined evidence on the spiritual Paracelsian Hamlet. On both Elizabethan and modern terms, Paul and Paracelsus have equal and parallel claims to priority in intellectual history as they also have been sustained from that era into ours. This chapter will redress the imbalance between Hamlet's harsh story and Shakespeare's spiritual cause. In addition, the chapter will address the balance between the certainty of Paul's Christian ethics and the mystery of Paracelsus's quintessential soul of the world entering every individual soul. We must go there because Shakespeare has borrowed both handles of his topsy-turvy metaphor of human nature from Phillipus Aureolus Theophrastus Bombastus von Hohenheim, hereinafter called Paracelsus (1493–1541), the father of modern holistic medicine.

We have reached a rare moment where the tally of the previous chapters has opened my readers to understand the distinguishing landscapes of the play and the separate agendas from within the minds of the protagonist and the manipulating dramatist. Thus we are ready to align learning with religion, Paracelsus with Paul, Hamlet's harsh story with the dramatist's spiritual path accessible to human nature. We can travel the spiritual journey of the play from the nadir in Act 2 to its sublimity in Act 5. In the play's dynamic interim from bestial low to potentially ascendant, human nature's destiny will either revert to crawling in the dust of chaos described in Genesis or soar heavenward through Paul's love thy neighbor and Paracelsus's quintessence.

As new modern options intruded, Elizabethans lived, like us, amidst a tangled web of new certainties and ambiguous mysteries that overlapping epistemologies in religion, learning, and art still attempt to elucidate for us today. As the dividend of fifteenth-century printing, the Christian religion in old and new dimensions brought on new certainties. Furthermore, classical learning fused religion with science to introduce startling new spiritual mysteries.

Sixteenth-century England stands out for gleaning new human directions from these two publishing milestones that examined spiritual causes from new perspectives. On one hand, the Reformation produced Englished bibles in Puritan, Anglican, and Catholic versions. They brought the Christian certainties of the innovative Paul into the ascendancy as we have seen as the theme of the first part of this book and where he remains. Shakespeare was able to integrate Paul's unambiguous Christian precepts in a new style revenge tragedy in *Hamlet* based on Romans 13.

On the other hand, the rise of natural philosophy and chemistry in the late Renaissance united the classical world and Christianity. That was the legacy of humanism. These disciplines brought the supernatural mysteries of the innovative Paracelsus, his empirical analysis, and his modern holistic medicine into the ascendancy. Complementing each other, Paul's "armour of lyght" and Paracelsus's *lumen naturae* both reflect divine celestial forces within us that are alternatingly clear and haunting (Rom. 13:12). In *Hamlet*, Shakespeare effects a total assimilation of Paul's communal religious grace and Paracelsus's alchemical quintessence, which when combined are a pivotal key to the play's spiritual blueprint and, in consequence, its architecture.

At the 1600 moment of *Hamlet*, Paul and Paracelsus were equally influential and in fashion in well-circulated books on religion and alchemy respectively; they would continue their leadership dominance in these distinct spiritual provinces throughout the seventeenth century. Now in our period they continue undiminished with seminal principles and horizon-oriented credentials; they are buttressed with solidly reinforced foundation stones and major avenues of spiritual innovation that remain in place.

How important is Paracelsus to Shakespeare? This clear challenger to the rational medicine of Galen linked the natural world of alchemy with the supernatural world of the Genesis creation myth in remarkable ways. Aware of the overlap, Shakespeare introduced Paracelsus silently like he had Paul in the 1600 *Hamlet*. Thus the earlier play anticipates alchemy as a major influence on his forthcoming 1606 *King Lear*.

In the 1606 *King Lear* which the 1600 *Hamlet* anticipates, the dramatist deals in characters caught in various stages between the nadir and zenith of three concentric wheels of fire, fortune, and generations. As we saw earlier in the play within the play, the Wheel of Fortune leads to a damnable nadir with no future. In *Lear,* the other two wheels can lead painfully to the zenith through alchemical transformation, but require utter destitution of the former self at the nadir of the wheels. "In Shakespeare's hands," says Charles Nicholl, "it is a process of spiritual growth . . . to attain [Paracelsian?] knowledge and [Pauline?] love" (Nicholl, *The Chemical Theatre* published by Routledge in 1980, 145). In both, the protagonist follows the thorny path in belated quest of the waking soul.

As with Paul and Christianity, we need ask how crucially pivotal was Paracelsus to the history of medicine from Galen to our era, the play, and to Shakespeare and his contemporaries. Above all, we must examine Paracelsus's seminal image of Plato's macrocosmic world soul, that is, quintessence, as it derives from the creation myth of Genesis and becomes the keystone of the play *Hamlet.*

It is now that penultimate moment to parse the extremely sophisticated, but the poet's profound metaphor for the species, "quintessence of dust." It is the neglected centerpiece of the play *Hamlet.* As a result of Paracelsus, seventeenth-century science adopted a corpuscular philosophy that added this fifth empirical humoral element to Galen's original rational four humors. Paracelsus has looked at the macrocosmic level for the unifying world soul and for its microcosmic correspondence in the human soul. Predominant for Paracelsus's philosophy and medicine is the idea of the 'Predestined Element' or 'Quinta Essentia.' "In each object one of the [four] humors [earth, water, fire, air] acquires a power superior to that of the other—and it is this element which forms the kernel of the object. It embodies all its specific power and virtues [arcana] and thereby marks the essential difference of one object from another" (Walter Pagel, *Paracelsus: An Introduction to Philosophical Medicine in the Era of the Renaissance*, Karger, 1982, 83). Matter or nature's raw stuff becomes vitally alive and capable when the individual rescues the spark of his own unique quintessence. Paracelsus and Shakespeare are attentive to the waking of the soul. Similarly in holistic medicine practiced today, the body knows better than the prescribing physician based on reading the symptomatology of the condition (which is a kind of quintessence) and the virtuous curative treatment (the arcana) becomes manifest by the patient consistent with the symptoms.

But first to return for the bad news, let us go backstage. In the last scene, the dying Hamlet asks Horatio twice to report "my cause aright to the unsatisfied" (5.2.341–2) and to "tell my story" (5.2.353) in this harsh world. Yet, if Hamlet, the audience, and the murderer concentrate only on Hamlet's stymied Roman old-style Senecan cause to revenge the murder of his father, a task occupying the entire play, they will continue to miss Shakespeare's subliminal spiritual cause. On one hand, Hamlet's story consists of cursed circumstances, nadirs in his own life, that he tries to make sense of through incisive soliloquies.

On the other hand, Shakespeare's profound humanistic cause, a substantial subtext, evaluates the universal spiritual path of human nature as a result of these two new, separate, but parallel developments in sixteenth-century religion and learning. He traces this state-of-the-art very methodically, assessing gains and losses through well-placed digressions. In the process, the play *Hamlet* joins together the transcendent spiritual causes of Paul and Paracelsus. Thus the play's entire infrastructure aligns Hamlet's harsh story with Shakespeare's spiritually-oriented, more lofty learned two-pronged cause.

It is no coincidence that this double infrastructure for the play, Hamlet's harsh story and Shakespeare's profound spiritual causes, mirror the double infrastructure of my own life and this book, my harsh twentieth-century story told objectively and my spiritual causes laid down subjectively in the macrocosmic interests as my 'part of the main.'

The Act 2 nadir of the play comes for both Hamlet and the dramatist either from despair of human nature in the play or in Europe characterized in the heretofore neglected and yet the play's most remarkable image, the "quintessence of dust." Hamlet runs the human spectrum:

> What a piece of work is a man! How noble in reason, how infinite in faculties, in form and moving how express and admirable, in action how like an angel, in apprehension how like a god! The beauty of the world, the paragon of animals! And yet, to me, what is this quintessence of dust? (2.2.304–309)

Shakespeare has poetically linked the unlinkable. Borrowed collectively from Plato's concept of the chemical world soul and the Old Testament creation myth by way of Paracelsus, the contradictory image, like the unpredictable fate of human nature at a new pivotal crisis, raises the potential of the species to achieve the sublime yet ends up, through misdeeds of the species, to the utter chaos before the Fall—a universe strewn with corpses.

Shakespeare first defines his own spiritual cause using these clashing Paracelsian key terms quintessence and dust ironically. The burden of his bad news inquiry? Whether our earthbound human nature is limited to the bestial activities of crawling in the primordial mud or whether we may yet soar spiritually heavenward to a divine calling by infusion of quintessence. Hamlet, unaware of his author's cause, becomes the test case for that larger horizon through an unending series of horrific events he fails to manage. He has become too obsessed with his revenge task. Thus in judging the antics of human nature, Hamlet has a glimmer of the extremes. He eloquently presents his pessimistic assessment despite his equally eloquent optimism.

The Wheel of Fortune is turning slowly downward. In Act 2, we are at this nadir, nonetheless, filled with ambiguity descending from the sublime celebration of God's greatest spiritual creation, then modulating to first among animals, but finally reduced in the Paracelsian key word vocabulary to an enigmatic afflicted species fallen from the heights to the lower depths. The purposeful opposition and merging of paragon and animal matches parallel tensions and merging of the equal, but contradicting opposites of quintessence and dust and of the independent vocabularies of alchemy and religion from which the words derive.

From the low point of the "quintessence of dust" in Act 2 to the play's spiritual sublime in Act 5, Hamlet is manipulated coordinately by the dramatist and "heaven ordinant"—*deus ex machina*—until his recognition that "the readiness is all" (5.2.48, 5.2.220). Readiness is the simple waking of the soul from the quintessence of dust to sublime quintessence. This attainment comes when he bids farewell to his own picayune revenge failures and submits to the divine plan of the godhead. Man without God is a failure.

Shakespeare's metaphor yokes the unlinkable. What is he doing? Juxtaposing Paracelsus's own concept of quintessence as the human zenith with his concept of dust in Genesis as the human nadir is a contradiction in chemical terms marking the vast difference between the untapped capacity of our spiritual natures and our fatal irredeemable tendencies. It is a bold dramatic stroke and the only time quintessence and dust are juxtaposed in their full meanings in all of Shakespeare. They are the opposite spiritual destinies of the play when Hamlet's own cause and his pessimism for human nature are simultaneously at their nadir. In a profound joining of seemingly incompatible definitions of our spiritual and bodily human natures, Shakespeare yokes and contrasts Paracelsus's two central images of his own alchemical concept of the divine quintessence and its antithesis of dust borrowed from Genesis.

More bad news. Paul's single Christian ethical principle to love thy neighbor rather than exploit him received unusual currency in the sixteenth century as the result of the English-language Bible in the wake of printing. But the coordinate discovery of the New World gave the impetus to global exploitation of Africans, Native Americans, and Asians by Europeans in a master/slave complex that will not go away. There is a new collective will. The fortune seekers in the play depend on the aura of rectitude, devotion's visage collectively hiding selfish intent. They eschew knowledge for comforting information and its twin misinformation. Hamlet's own joy is satirizing their soulless emptiness and recording the perdition of collective corpses.

A new material world of empire building was on offer at the time that would ultimately broaden the base of wealth and power of a new elite not unlike the toadies around Claudius. No matter the new intellectual energies, the unending new discoveries, inventions, and mysteries on land and at sea threatened the old stable institutions and refused to be denied leadership maneuverability. By 1611 after Galileo's telescope overturned certainties in the heavens, John Donne confirmed that this new world was again a tangled web threatening European alliance of church and state. A new found individualism defined a new fragmented world. Poetry ran up against an irresistible tide.

> 'Tis all in pieces, all coherence gone.
> All just supply, and all relation:
> Prince, subject, father, son are things forgot,
> For every man alone thinks he has got
> To be a phoenix, and that then can be
> None of that kind of which he is, but he.
> "Anniversaries," 213–18

Donne foresaw a seismic cultural shift in Europe from communal spiritual growth to individual material gains. Hamlet belonged to the old stultifying royal courtier tradition. Although tangentially transfixed, he was abreast of the new humanistic learning which he wanted to get on with at Wittenberg.

With the somber metaphor, quintessence of dust, epistemology looms as a problem. Knowledge systems have separate vocabularies. Before tackling dust in this human nature formula, therefore, let us examine more intricately the Paracelsian and Shakespearian vital key word quintessence with all its cognates first and definitions later. Quintessence, a chemical concept associating our microcosmic world with Plato's divine macrocosm, matches the Holy Spirit of the Trinity as the special linking with the Christian God. In turn, they both match the Greek concept of *agape*, the divine love that enters our souls when they become a receiving vessel.

Whatever area of sophisticated knowledge, ancient or modern, we employ, the key issue comes down to proofs for or against supernatural intervention in human affairs and the tenuousness of our access to these mysterious divine forces. As with Paul, the relation of the mind to the body, the interactions between them, the connection of the whole individual to God, gods, divine and/or natural and supernatural forces cross many knowledge systems since the Reformation and the rise of science. Nomenclature alone can become unwieldy when we call the mind or the individual's communication with the outside world as soul or the unconscious, either rational or feeling.

The problem becomes daunting when we need to combine overlapping or contradictory contributions with inexact denominators in no sequential order from religion and philosophy alongside alchemy, chemistry and psychoanalysis. When we enter the spiritual realm, the mysteries become compounded by speculation and lack of confirmation about "the undiscover'd country [death] from whose bourn / No traveller returns" (3.1.80–81). Also key words in one discipline could substitute as keys to another. Soul and the unconscious could have multiple interpretations or specialized meanings confusing the original definitions and with each other. If we ask where to find the generative influence separating celestial souls from gross bodies, lines are blurred.

Shakespeare's dedication to, and fascination with, Paracelsus in sixteen of his plays has been fully documented in Charles Nicholl's *The Chemical Theatre*. What did his contemporaries say about quintessence? Nicholl quotes John Dee, who refers to Our Mercury, the Quintessence, as the celestial messenger "drawing down the life of heaven," an influx of heavenly powers into earthly matter (47). Dee's "talismanic synopsis of the alchemical process" gives Our Mercury the central place "primarily symbolic of the quintessential spirit within matter" (45). Are we not close to that immortal ninth-century Pentecostal hymn "*Veni Creator Spiritus*," still among us with its thrust intact despite harmonic changes? Consider the 1905 Robert Bridges translation:

> Come, O Creator Spirit, come
> And make within our hearts thy home:
> To us thy Grace celestial give,
> Who of thy breathing move and live.
> (Hymn 48)

The notion of linking or knitting together heaven and earth with a golden thread, or divine fifth element, has occupied religion, alchemy, and poetry separately; and these affinities about spiritual matters, especially of accessibility to an overarching universal harmony, occasion borrowings in concept and language from each other. Indeed, the preface to George Ripley's 1591 *Compound of Alcymy* reverberates with quintessence in the mode of the poets:

> [Quintessence] is a Soule, a substance bright;
> Of Sunne and Moone a subtill influence,
> Whereby the earth receiveth resplendence.
> (quoted in Nicholl, 36)

That we find quintessence experienced everywhere in the two decades surrounding 1600, Nicholl points out, may be attributed ironically to its definition as "infused into everything." "Nature" wrote Paracelsus,

> is not visible, though it operates visibly; for it is simply a volatile spirit, fulfilling its office in bodies, and animated by the universal spirit—the divine breath, the central and universal fire, which vivifies all things that exist.
> (quoted in Nicholl, 3)

The 1597 *Mirror of Alchimy* alludes to matter invested with supernatural properties of harmony, incorruptibility, and spirituality such as the Philosopher's Stone, elixir, or philosopher's gold which could be paraphrased quintessence in dust (Nicholl, 32).

Initially the dramatist faces a daunting problem to align the separate conceptual terminologies in the Christian religion and classical learning. This recurring epistemological stymie of different learned vocabularies is one Paracelsus, Shakespeare, and generations of humanists, in turn, have had to surmount. We also must remember that, though the term quintessence is alchemically-specific, the fifteenth-century Florentine Neoplatonists Marsilio Ficino and Pico della Mirandola, pivotally influenced Paracelsus, performing their own fusing of Plato and Christianity.

What we have here with Shakespeare and Paracelsus using the same biblical and chemical sources interchangeably to deal with spiritual issues has been an endemic problem since the early Renaissance. Dante had this problem in *The Divine Comedy* and we do today. Dante's issue was: Where do you put the giants of classical secular learning whose universal findings either relate, remain ambiguous, challenge, encroach, accommodate or overlap with Christianity? Dante created the artificial first circle as a halfway house for them between philosophy and religion.

Paracelus himself could not escape the same problem of nomenclature. He yoked disparate knowledge categories in linking heaven and earth by means of chemistry and alchemy, the creation myth in Genesis and Neoplatonism. In the process, he encroached with his own myth of a new fifth element, quintessence, that surpassed the bodily and psychiatric healing properties of the other four classical humors: earth, air, fire, and water. Paracelsus calibrated human nature on a spectrum ranging to its zenith heaven by quintessence and to its nadir earthbound by dust, our low life epitome as defined in Genesis. Shakespeare brilliantly and bafflingly links these two Paracelsian words in his most pivotal, ironic, and eloquent passage on his cause to indicate the outer limits of how high human nature may soar and how low we may crawl.

It is time to look at the other handle of the metaphor of human nature. Dust presents fewer verbal problems than its metaphoric twin. Next to fortune, dust is Shakespeare's most recurring image in the play of how low we may sink given half a chance. The sophisticated reach of this weird alignment would only have been savored by an intellectual elite in his day and a handful of historians of alchemy and medical science in ours.

Hamlet's "quintessence of dust" human epitome ironically drops us from the sublime possibility to the equal ambiguity of alchemy's and Genesis's mean reality. God in Genesis gave man dominion over all living creatures and inspired into man's "nostrylles the breath of lyfe" (Gen. 2:7). "What," asks "is Life itself, but as it is commonly called, the *Breath* of our nostrils?" (Cf. John Milton, *Paradise Lost*, 7.524-527: "This said, he formed thee, Adam, thee O Man / Dust of the ground, and in thy nostrils breathed / The breath of life; in his own Image he / Created thee," 177).

No biblical image is stronger in the play than dust, which Shakespeare bequeaths to Hamlet in full measure. It is a metaphor that, like breath, carries both alchemical quintessence and religious grace. In Genesis 2 before the Fall we learn that "The Lorde God also dyd shape man even dust from of the grounde and breathed into his nostrylles the breath of lyfe, and man was a living soul" (Gen. 2:7)

In Genesis 3 after the Fall we learn that "In the sweat of thy face shalt thou eate thy bread, til thou be turned agayne into the grounde, for out of it were thou taken: for dust thou art, and into dust shalt thou be turned agayne" (Gen. 3:19). Recall, "who would fardels [i.e. bundles, burdens, and misfortunes] bear" in Hamlet's soliloquy on the calamities of existence, followed by his fixation on dust (3.1.77). What has he done with Polonius's body? "Compounded it with dust, whereto 'tis Kin" (4.2.7).

And what of the noble dust of Alexander and Caesar, who bestrode the ancient world priding themselves on their divinity? In the gravedigger's scene Hamlet ponders "to what base uses we may return" (5.1.202) "Alexander returneth to dust, the dust is earth, of earth we make loam, and why of that loam might they not stop a beer barrel" (5.1.209–212). No less does Imperial Caesar receive his due: "Oh that that earth, which kept the world in awe, / Should patch a wall, t'expell the winter's flaw" (5.1.215–216)

There is a need to digress on Paracelsus's reputation in Elizabethan and modern times. Long before Shakespeare's daughter married a Paracelsian physician, the dramatist, as well as his contemporaries the metaphysical poet John Donne and the skeptical philosopher Montaigne, revered the Paracelsian spiritual vocabulary as having become sacrosanct throughout continental Europe by the time of Paracelsus's death in 1541. Although he used Paracelsian concepts more conspicuously in his later plays after that marriage, the medical scientist's key term quintessence unlocks many doors to Shakespeare's private causes in conceiving the play *Hamlet*.

Paracelsus's career and reputation remain more checkered than Paul's, but equally mesmerizing then and now. His wide ranging humanism ventured along new pathways extending from substantial chemical experimentation and myriads of conceptual therapeutic breakthroughs to highly imaginative, yet pregnant speculation on metaphysical spiritual mysteries connected with a more intricate anatomy and stirrings in psychiatry under the then burgeoning natural philosophy and alchemy.

Such speculation in alchemy and miracles, however, drew in collections of mountebanks deservedly unspared in the savage satires employing Galen's classical humoral traditions in literature and medicine by Ben Jonson in Shakespeare's day and Jonathan Swift a century later. These satiric bullseyes did not deter alchemy at its scientific and spiritual core as the basis for modern Jungian psychoanalysis, a clear departure from Freud. I have published on his dual positive and negative legacies (Cf: Craven's chapter on Parcelsus in *Jonathan Swift and the Millenium of Madness*).

These profound attacks implicating Paracelsus did not dim his medical influence today either. His empiric holistic and integrated medicine continues as the one serious challenge to rationalistic Galenic humoral tradition; they are the two available medical treatments when we see our doctor at present. The physician either employs Galen by attacking the invading disease with drugs or surgery or the Paracelsian holistic treatment that assumes the body connected to some higher force knows best how to administer to itself. Often the modern doctor at his wit's end and tries both. Paracelsus's integrated medicine is still at the pioneer borders of global change today.

Strangely Paracelsus gets another boost in editions of the play after 1603. To integrate Paracelsus into the play, Shakespeare introduced his medical and biblical terminology, changing the word 'God' in the first 1603 quarto to 'heaven' throughout the second 1604 quarto, and aligned Pauline and Paracelsian optimism as the action moved at a snail's pace from nadirs of gloom to epiphanies of divine intervention.

Regarding the shift in terms, I cannot prove that the changes were made solely to accommodate Paracelsus. In a more balanced view, Andrew Gurr points out that:

> Quarto 1 represents a very crude and largely memorial transcript of the play as acted in the first years. Quarto 2 … is based on the version as staged, probably with changes introduced as late as 1620. Your evidence about changes in naming 'gods' or 'God' and 'heaven' doesn't take account of the 1606 Act to restrain abuses in playhouses, which imposed a fine of 10£ for taking God's name in vain, and led to a widespread modification of the texts, often inserting the moderate 'heavens' instead of the deity's name. (personal correspondence with the author, 24 March, 1993).

What takes place spiritually from Act 2 to Act 5 that transforms Hamlet to quintessence? Hamlet's story—and by extension, the audience's—hinges on obedience to earthly or divine power: a human choice. One cannot imagine any of his opposers concluding as Hamlet does that his "dear soul [is] mistress of her choice" (3.2.62). But if we accept for the moment Elizabethan ideas of divine right, then his royal or temporal duty cannot be separated from the issue of his soul. Laertes warns Ophelia that on Hamlet's "choice depends / The safety and health of this whole state"—to wit, its heaven and earth (1.3.20–21). The audience's choice is less clear cut: Paul's civic duty and one's soul.

Shakespeare has very neatly presented the audience closure on both these options. Look at what is left us after the dust settles in Denmark. Has anything changed? The beginning and end of the play, like dust to dust, tell us that after the disruption of the regicide, the state will again be feudal business as usual. At the outset, Hamlet's Ghost clanks about in his armor; and when it is over, the militant Fortinbras, his father's clone, fed with the absess "of much wealth and peace" (4.4.28) exposes "what is mortal and unsure [20,000 soldiers] / To all that fortune, death, and danger dare, / Even for an eggshell"—a little patch of unfarmable ground in Poland

(4.4.52–54). On the civic side of things, therefore, in spite of Hamlet's successful revenge at the play's end, we have merely returned to the stabilized martial feudalism of his father where honor and aggrandizement are inextricably intertwined. If this is all that Hamlet's little breath has restored to statehood, what then has his breath achieved in his personal interval from dust to dust? Only a spiritual answer to this question, which turns classical revenge tragedy on its head, can justify his "story."

Whatever his labeling, Shakespeare sets up a fundamental opposition between this chancy world and sure eternity. On one scale, we have the natural matters within the observable and measureable province of science and reportage. On the other scale we have the supernatural within the recondite and immeasurable province of alchemy, religion, art, and the occult. While Shakespeare cultivates an ambiguity among the practitioners within each province as he does among worshippers in the distinct Christian sects, his distinctions between provinces remain sacrosanct. It is as if he has accepted the alchemical separation of the bodily and spiritual aspects of matter: the vital essence of quintessence. At the same time he has placed on his tragic hero the weight of Paul's exhortation to the Romans in chapter 12, verses 1 and 2:

> [Geve] up your bodyes a quicke sacrifice, holy, acceptable unto God, which is your reasonable service. And be not ye fashioned lyke unto this World: *but* be ye changed in your shape, by the renuying of your mynde (Rom. 12:1–2)

Yet we come to Shakespeare's startling separation of religion and chemistry in the text. We can now see how Shakespeare modulates the certainties of Paul's religion with the ambiguities of Paracelsus's alchemical chemistry. That Paracelsus and Paul receive equal, but separate billing, we need only turn to the play's so-called "bad," or pirated, first quarto of 1603 to understand how he anticipates both the more dramatically and poetically enriched second quarto of 1604–1605 and the seamless 1623 folio. From the first and second quarto to the first folio, we witness almost uniformly a consistent change from the word "God" to the word "heaven." Bertram and Kliman's 1991 *Three-Text Hamlet,* with these earlier texts aligned in parallel on facing pages, greatly simplifies our peering over the shoulder of the master of connotative ambiguity and total assimilation at his work.

"For God's love" in the first and second quarto becomes "For Heaven's love" in the first folio (Bertram and Kliman, Q1&2.386, F1.1.2.195); similarly, "O God" twice turns into "Oh Heaven" (Q1&2.709, F1.1.5.24). The oath "Jesus" in 1603 becomes "Oh heavens" in 1604;

while the oath "Great God of heaven" in 1603 is excised by 1604 (Q1.920). The 1603 "Why what's the matter?" changes to "With what in the name of God" in 1604 and finally to "With what in the name of Heaven?" in 1623 (Q1.970, Q2.972, F1.2.1.73). In the 1603 version, Ophelia prays "Help him, good God" (Q1.1789). And finally in 1623, "O heavenly Powers, restore him" (F1.3.1.141). There is further studied ambiguity as Shakespeare changes Ophelia's remembrance of Hamlet's vows in each recension. The 1603 "earnest vowes" become "holy vowes of heaven" in 1604, and finally in 1623, "vowes of heaven" (Q1.580, Q2.580, F1.1.3.114).

God and heaven, religion and alchemy are intertwined in a 1603 passage that becomes more focused and identifiable in both areas by 1604. "O that this too much grieved and sallied flesh would melt to nothing, or that the universal globe of heaven would turn all to a chaos! O God within two months married" (Q1.1.2.202–205). By 1604 Hamlet's pre-Genesis wish is more precise; "that this too too sallied flesh would melt, / Thaw and resolve it selfe into a dewe" (Q2.1.2.313–314). Note that Shakespeare has withdrawn Hamlet's imploring an ambiguous "globe of heaven," not God, to reverse Genesis and restore chaos, a nadir lower than his "quintessence of dust" epitome.

Essentially, the first quarto, accentuating "nothing" and "chaos," finds Hamlet advocating an empty nihilism. In all subsequent editions, Hamlet insists on reversal of the Genesis myth, not its enhancement. "Solid" becomes "sullied" (defiled) and nature becomes "an unweeded garden" (Bevington and Kastan, 1.2.129, 135).

In all versions of the play, quintessence has not entered into Hamlet's head in Act 1. Shakespeare, in contrast already has introduced his audience to the positive alchemical reading of Genesis, thus anticipating his use of quintessence. In the second quarto, he accentuates "melt, thaw and resolve into a dew," presenting Paracelsus's quintessential alchemical spirit as liberating Hamlet from raw matter, "this too, too sullied flesh," by the alchemist's dissolving process (1.2.129–130). The spiritual transformation desired resounds with alchemical sulphur and Our Mercury or quintessence: the former, solid and bodily; the latter, moist, vaporous, spiritual, a spirit inside matter (See the earlier discussion on page 81). Nicholl clinches this discussion on the alchemical-biblical associations of "dew:"

> "The *ros caeli* or 'dew of heaven' [in Genesis]...suggests Our Mercury, variously described in alchemical writings as 'divine rain,' 'silver rain,' 'drop of wet dew,' etc."
> (Nicholl, 46)

Shakespeare's feat is to move from the crimes of violence and passion so characteristic of the earlier revenge plays—as they continue in the entertainment and real life mayhem atop our current media charts—to make of the unwitting Hamlet by a series of epiphanies, a king, a minister of grace, and a waking soul immortal. When he despairingly mocks undelightful man and woman too, and also the inspirational hope of alchemy and the Bible, with that epitome of both sexes as "Quintessence of dust," he and we are still at this juncture of the play under the spell of an irredeemable and spiritually cut-off earth. We are in a feudal environment haunted by devils and witches by night and rife with villains and timeservers tyrannizing the weary and sorely oppressed by day.

It is now high time to move rationally from his nadirs at the play's outset to Hamlet's epiphanies that justify Shakespeare's humanistic causes and echo mine. Shakespeare's independent spiritual causes in religion and chemistry work by stages and enlightened me to unique frames of reference to unravel *Hamlet*. Insisting that we live in a harsh world insures that the dramatist and I, his pedestrian sojourner, will always set the record straight by releasing the bad news first—the nadir of defeated expectation—before the best news can attain any legitimate standing—the epiphany of divine spiritual intervention. To set the record straight, I, too, believe that the relation of the past to the future functions outside the fashion of the present. Like all media, the dramatist fastens on a particular in the public eye at the moment. But Shakespeare sweeps the temper of the time into the universal realm of systemic change, my engineering specialty, where history past and change in the future come together.

But these cosmic horizons require verifiable knowledge as my cross-disciplinary encyclopedic knowledge systems confirm. In the meantime, historical continuity limps in a partisan present dominated by the inseparable pair: information and misinformation. As one of the founding fathers of the first schools of information and computer science with doctoral programs in the early 1960s, I speak with authority on all programmed information as increasingly technically shortsighted on transparency and adept on raising material, not spiritual, expectations. On his say so, Polonius convinces Claudius that Hamlet's antics stem from love and not purposed mystification. Ophelia feigns piety; Rosencranz and Gildenstern feign friendship. Only Horatio meets the standard acceptable to the dramatist, Hamlet and me in this harsh misinformed, groveling world. Trust no one who can't be trusted in everything. In the play, only Horatio meets this exacting standard. In an epitome of his friend who has escaped fortune's meddlesome finger, Hamlet exclaims, "Give me that man / That is not passion's slave, and I will wear him / In my heart's core" (3.2.70–72). It should be a primary principle of learning in a seamy age.

To set the record straight on this exacting standard for trust, the dramatist and I search all occasions for epitomes and epiphanies which often turn up in pairs. For example, the single device of spying from a secret perch epitomizes Lord Burghley's, a.k.a. Polonius's, strategems and shifty character throughout the Tudor reign. An epiphany comes unbidden for Hamlet when he slays Polonius behind the arras. Divine forces have, as he relates, punished both Polonius and him in one stroke. The opposite of an epiphany is a nadir that Claudius experiences when his prayers do not go up to heaven. He is already the incapacitated living dead, cut off from God. The play irrevocably reverses roles piling up nadirs for evil doers and epiphanies for those with spiritual initiatives. It is helpful to contrast Hamlet's use of quintessence of dust in what seems like a disparaging context of man, alchemy, religion, and all human fate in Act 2 and the idea of quintessence as a "restoration…to perfect temper" (Nicholl 30) exemplified in the spritual Hamlet's confident "the readiness is all" in Act 5.

Shakespeare's neat division of the play at this climactic juncture—the death of Polonius—goes to the transformation in Hamlet as his mindset mutes the themes of the enormity of evil everywhere and the enormity of his lonely task to his soul's acceptance of Horatio's assurance to Marcellus at the play's outset: "Heaven will direct it" (1.4.91) Thus what seems diversionary and irrelevant to the audience bent on closure of the revenge, such as the passage to England, the graveside scene, and the duel, do not try Hamlet's patience similarly. Confirming Horatio's reassurance to the audience earlier that "heaven will direct," Hamlet announces "heaven ordinant" in all his seeming diversionary actions. As he had felt darkness, futility, and despair until the murder of Polonius, so for the balance of the play he quotes liberally from Matthew on heaven's omnipresence in human affairs. Not a sparrow falls to the ground without God's knowing it (Matthew 10:29). The readiness is all in doing what heaven has prepared for us: "When our deep plots do pall, and that should learn us / There's a divinity that shapes our end, / Rough-hew them how we will" (5.2.9–11). Readiness is simply quintessence in operation.

When Hamlet and his audience focus on revenge and Hamlet, more than the audience, becomes distracted with his personal focus on actual death and living deaths, audiences and critics tend to label his latter obsession lily-livered and dishonorable indecision. But Shakespeare uses this seeming diversion as the fundamental engine for transforming *Hamlet*, once predictable revenge tragedy, and the audience, only perhaps, to an entirely other plane of perception where all decisive human actions must undergo prior spiritual scrutiny. Here is Shakespeare's bargain not to be only the soul of the age, but a literary artist for all time. In the medieval mystery plays, delight was not sacrificed to instruction and Christian dogmas or Catholic rites were not insisted on. In moving from the specifics of God and his judgments in the 1603 quarto to the term heaven and to alchemical allusions in the 1604 quarto, Shakespeare has consciously yoked the spiritual forces of the Bible with alchemical learning familiar to Catholics, Anglicans, and Puritans.

If Hamlet's "inky blackness" alone did not deter him, even after the unimpeachable proof of the mousetrap play, Hamlet's imperative to kill Claudius is circled round with mixed messages in myriad Church doctrines, dogma, and rites, with admixtures of hobgoblin lore and civil injunctions, importing that "the cess of majesty / Dies not alone" (3.3.15–16)—all restraints incorporated in "that monster custome" (Q2.2544+1). Neither heavenly alchemy nor divine judgment, that is, quintessence nor inspiriting of the dust, figure in his human equation before the epiphany in Act 5.

The transformation of Hamlet and revenge tragedy modulates from the moment Claudius falls on his knees admitting to himself that his offence "hath the primal eldest curse upon't" and that "Pray can I not" (3.3.37–38). Stymied from classical revenge when he finds Claudius at prayer, Hamlet simultaneously ticks off the litany of religious restraints, mouths all the thundering rhetoric of classical revenge, and stalks into his mother's chamber in high dudgeon. In less than a minute, he has committed impulsive, passion-inspired bloody, earth-bound revenge within the classical tradition, albeit mistakenly on Polonius. Only after a protracted castigation of his mother, during which the ghost drops by to warn him of "thy almost blunted purpose" (3.4.115), does Hamlet, passion spent, pause to sort out the spiritual meaning of his murdering the wrong victim. It is the pivotal passage when he acknowledges, on one hand, his own sinful act as heaven's scourge or agent and recognizes, on the other, for the first time in the play a new, divinely-ordained role outside classical revenge as heaven's minister or instrument. "I do repent; but heaven hath pleased it so, / To punish me with this, and this with me, / That I must be their scourge and minister…This bad begins, and worse remains behind" (3.4.180–186).

Eminent modern Shakespeareans from Fredson Bowers to Northrup Frye have also recognized the Pauline source for Christian revenge that moves beyond the Judeo-Christian edict "Vengeance is mine, I will repay saith the Lord" (Rom. 12:19). As we developed earlier, it is in the second of a pair of chapters (12–13) in his Epistle to the Romans setting down our practical civil duties. These chapters as a unit concern duties to civil rulers and Romans 13:4 advises that the ruler "is the minister of God to thee for good. But if thou do that which is evil; be afraid for he beareth not the sword in vain; for he is the minister of God, a revenger to execute wrath upon him that doeth evil."

Let us end on a modern note. Psychoanalysis is one of the great developments in an otherwise warlike century. Therefore, I am giving Sigmund Freud and Karl Jung the last words in this chapter. While Freud's interest in the unconscious concentrated on the inner self, Jungians, on the other hand, emphasized the collective unconscious, or how we behave collectively as a species. Consequently, I am a Freudian as far as the unconscious in individual clinical practice, but a Jungian when it comes to the unconscious of the species in intellectual history. Ironically, Freud's general pessimism about unconscious primal motives and conscious patriarchal tyrannies, those hierarchies, and about our fatal destiny, has sparked critics like Karen Horney and Erich Fromm to argue for the possibilities of individual social goodness, decency, and growth, based on peaceful virtues.

The Jungians have created a more scientific and universal road between Freud's pessimism and that of his critics, and my optimism. Any perusal of Nicholl's book *The Chemical Theatre* devoted to Shakespeare's wide use of the alchemy of Paracelsus will find his wide dependence on Jung as an articulate bridge between Elizbethan and our understanding of the unconscious. Paracelsus, Shakespeare, and Jung linked chemistry and religion. Jung called alchemy the undercurrent to Christianity. To quote Jung, church ritual and dogma "alienated consciousness from its natural roots in the unconscious" psyche (Nicholl, 5). To paraphrase Nicholl, the entirety of our physical nature, our raw stuff, Hamlet's 'solid flesh,' was animated by the quintessence within, a manifestation of the universal *anima mundi*. The alchemist reiterated the Creation itself.

In 1993, I was asked to prepare an essay review of Marie-Luise von Franz's final work, *Psyche and Matter* (1992), a collection of essays summing up Jungian contributions to intellectual history and psychoanalysis, for the history of chemistry journal *Ambix* (41:96–7). Von Franz was distinguished as Jung's intellectual equal, colleague, collaborator, and successor. Her three-column *New York Times* March 23, 1998 obituary characterized her as the compassionate and effective queen of Jungian psychology, a legend who had studied fairy tales universally as the world of the unconscious, analyzed over 65,000 dreams, and made Jungian work increasingly her own.

For von Franz, humans can't get at the great collective truths about our God-created world because they are bogged down in conscious reality with false knee-jerk ethical and critical attitudes. For instance, we believe so strongly in established laws and in mechanical cause and effect, the scientific attitude, that today's world will not allow God to be creative. Religious fundamentalism also replaces God's creativity with dogmatic human interpretation of His purposes. Following Jung in writing this book, I have had to postpone conscious reality in order to discover my unconscious. I have had to rethink what I do normally. For example, I finally realized that the plays with male leads or isolates that I conjured up as the only male teacher at St. Mary's Hall preparatory school for young women were unconscious attempts to restore normal binary gender relationships: systemic change. My unconscious saw me as the isolated male out of my element. I was literally drowning like the last man in that Synge play *Riders to the Sea* in a metaphorical sea of women. St. Mary's Hall could accommodate only one gender.

Like the myths of Adam and Eve and Noah's ark, we all think unconsciously in binaries. Consequently, for Jung, odd and even numbers are the most basic order of the human mind, the genetic code and the binary system of computers and all information. For Jung and for this chapter, the number two has become more important irrationally and qualitatively to my unconscious psyche, which directed all my traffic at St. Mary's.

Nothing happens mechanically. Like thinking unconsciously in a binary system of only two numbers, time as event oriented also is much more critical to Jung. Similarly, this first memoir and answer for our era is Jungian in presenting unconscious reality as the major determinant of our world. Nothing happens by chance. Thought of in Jungian terms, all time is a qualitatively characterized synchronist stream of unconscious events, no single moment of which happens by purely conscious accident. For example, when in college, I consciously rejected Irene Selznick's bounteous offer to live in and guide her sons in the New York and Hollywood entertainment environment for the temporary wealth of the New York Upper Eastside. When that one-year picnic was over, my unconscious took me by the hand without any clear conscious direction from me. It said, "Look here. You've been flirting with the New York entertainment industry ever since you were a kid. Sign up for dramatic arts in graduate school and follow your star." I only learned while writing this book what my unconscious was actually doing with the seeming conscious accidents of time during my life. Thus, in retrospect, my finally examined life becomes a beautiful tapestry woven out of my unconscious timing and is appropriate to my time and space, instead of the result of sheer randomness: a Hamlet or Lear journey on the wheels of fire and generations.

According to von Franz, thinking outside the conscious box, which this book ironically consciously does, illuminates our universal existence, our interdependent 'being a part of the main.' The idea is not new. John Donne says succinctly "no man is an island….Each man's death diminishes me" (Donne, *Devotions Upon Emergent Occasions*, 97). Since we're all connected, God, too, is important to Jungians because they see a great holistic Paracelsian design in the universe matched by a corresponding design in every individual life. We keep thinking in twos. There is, on one hand, matter or the Great Mother, and, on the other, psyche or the Great Father. The universal idea is more scientifically basic than naughty Adam and Eve who prance around Eden getting into mischief. These mythical naïfs cover their bodies (matter) with fig leaves, while they are oblivious to their souls (psyches). Once again, we come back to fusion of body and soul. As my experience establishes, that idea is at the heart of both the entertainment industry (boy meets girl) and all religions (the wedding covenant). These opposites, like all opposites in nature, wish to coalesce in a mysterious conjunction, recognizing their mutual 'influenceability,' the unity of being, and the oneness of the world.

Since she knew that I was not a Jungian, von Franz's unsolicited response to my review gave me great joy: "My heartiest thanks for your understanding review. I never even hoped for such a good review" (personal communication with the author). On September 5, 1994, Marie-Luise von Franz and I met at her home in Kusnacht on Lake Zurich in Switzerland. Like my one transfixed meeting with Irene Selznick a half-century earlier, there were long silences and keen unspoken mutual understandings between us. Her book and my review had already said it all. We had coalesced. If there was a mutual lament, it was that the stabilizing virtues had little currency now and that the planet was left to mediocrity that would never rise above conspiracies of human limitation, that is, conscious reality. With our own time measured, our separate legacies would be left in the sanctuary of the public domain. For me, these two meetings of unconscious reality with Selznick and von Franz, half a century apart, had brought me full circle. Our lives had been devoted to waking the soul, privately and collectively.

But I have been blessed with other epiphanies turning up when least expected and most needed. In arguing for the spiritual mysteries in religion and alchemy, we have slighted their revelatory equal in poetry. Once upon a time, in a harsh world, a saint from a time of poets entered my life, holding up a magic lantern. On his way home he stopped just long enough to guide some innocents lost in that darkness on how to recognize pure alchemical gold and thence to make their own way home with dignity and grace. The dark time was the spring of 1948 when the Soviets stole the nuclear secrets and thus began the Cold War. The innocents were about 20 of us Columbia College seniors, mostly hardened veterans of the Depression and World War II, who had signed up for an untaxing course in poetry, a respite in a brutal century as we eased toward graduation. We had no inkling of the hard facts. Actually, instead, we had signed up for a final, life-changing course offered by Raymond "Buck" Weaver, then dying of cancer, an outcast among his egotistical Ivy establishment peers since 1921, a year before my birth. Yet, Weaver was a remarkable teacher of essential human values for these same overly proud Ivy League peers, and a lonely beacon for undergraduate future stars.

Weaver had a thunderous voice and glaring steely eyes beneath fierce eyebrows. Joseph Mazzeo, the distinguished Dantean scholar, caught the constant electricity in his classroom: "The interminable silence as he waited for an answer; his gentleness if the answer was honest and inadequate; the capital punishment, if it sounded perverse or vain." What Weaver instilled was Dante's liberal education, missing in today's world, of instantly rewarding the seven peaceful virtues and punishing the seven meddlesome vices beginning with pride. Aesthetic and ethical values go hand in hand and require no less daily discipline than we assign unhesitatingly to bodily development. Art and the arts of living and dying provide meaning to every human encounter.

Among his rare disciples, Allen Ginsberg chose Weaver over Mark Van Doren as his favorite teacher. Van Doren's 1968 autobiography and Weaver's own writings on Herman Melville illustrate their Columbia departmental rivalry from 1921 to 1948 and Weaver's ultimate triumph over his illustrious rival and the usual diet of pedestrian professional fare passed off in the best learned circles.

In the 1920s, Van Doren and a host of Ivy League colleagues reveled in downgrading Weaver privately for his "precious, labored style." Yet Weaver's 1935 Introduction to Melville's *Journal Up the Straits* sets the artistic goal for this book. I, too, would like to "inspire in a reader the serenity and the exultation of wonder." But Weaver taught Van Doren and those of us listening something even more important than literature as a work of art: What does it mean that one's life must also be a work of art? Van Doren in 1968: "He disciplined me in courtesy, purely by his example—a work of art which his beloved Renaissance writers had assisted him to finish and perfect." Weaver projected beauty of soul, inherent thoughtfulness, humility, grace, a sense of what is right, considerate compassion, and kindness. The human art takes discipline to come at Buck Weaver's charm, manner, decency, regard for others, serenity, and sense of wonder.

Why did Weaver tower above his contemporaries? Faculty, students, and consumers want packaged deals. We all judge by auspices. Who said it? Where do you come from? What are your affiliations? Who but a Weaver would deny us this universal safety net for pigeon-holing our prideful opinions, our obsessions, pre-judgments, and prejudices?

Each class consisted of examining one poem without attribution. Never mind who wrote it or when or where. What does it say to enrich our lives? Everyone had to take a crack at it. Slowly its monumental specific gravity emerged. Like weight lifters, we were gradually developing new tough critical fibers to move from judging based on our humdrum mediocrity to the sublime platform of art. We analyzed untagged works from Wyatt to e.e. cummings, from Marvell to Emily Dickinson, from Blake to Marianne Moore, from Donne to Yeats. We began to realize that great poetry, if you could plumb it, opened you to rare profound truth you could trust in a century gone mad with technology, genocide, and war.

Ironically, Buck's infinite wisdom remains intact here. For our mid-term we each wrote a poem which led him to call me into his office and startle me. "Craven, you should write." I confronted him. "You told us, no one should write." His rejoinder was scolding and emphatic. "You didn't *listen*. I said no one should write unless he can't *help* it." I am listening now. The gracious and exacting Weaver has had the courtesy and patience to wait me out these sixty-three years.

What did Weaver see then that made him compare me with Hart Crane? In retrospect, my greatest gift is my profound analysis of the totality of the individual and our culture, as distinct from the misleading visible fragments usually on display. I've been particularly successful in connecting my seemingly unrelated careers: inter-disciplinary learning including classical drama, psychoanalytic psychotherapy practice and corporate infrastructure. In every instance, I've spent decades integrating very high levels of education, training, and leadership practice. I've written extensively on literature, history, science, medicine, philosophy, religion, and popular sovereignty. Yet I could not write a poem of such limpid beauty that defines us all on leaving. That Elizabethans understood certainties and mysteries in *Hamlet* better than we, Thomas Nashe echoes in the exquisite song from his own 1600 play, *Summer's Last Will and Testament*:

> Haste, therefore, each degree,
> To welcome destiny:
> Heaven is our heritage,
> Earth but a player's stage:
> Mount we unto the sky.
> I am sick, I must die.
> Lord have mercy on us!

Bibliography

Bertram, Paul, and Bernice W. Kliman, eds. *The Three-Text Hamlet: Parallel Texts of the First and Second Quartos and First Folio*. New York: AMS Press, 1991.

Bridges, Robert Seymour and Harry Ellis Wooldridge, eds. *Hymns: The Yattendon Hymnal.* Oxford: B. H. Blackwell, 1905.

Craven, John P. *The Silent War: The Cold War Battle Beneath the Sea.* New York: Simon & Schuster, 2002.

Craven, Kenneth. *Jonathan Swift and the Millenium of Madness: The Information Age in* 'A Tale of a Tub.' Leiden: E. J. Brill, 1992, and Lincoln, NE: iUniverse, 2006.

—. "Oedipus complex" and "Senex amator." In *Dictionary of Literary Themes and Motifs*. Edited by Jean-Charles Seigneuret. Westport, CT: Greenwood Press, 1988.

Craven, Kenneth and Leonard Cohan. *Science Information Personnel: The New Profession of Information.* New York: Modern Language Association of America and National Science Foundation, 1961.

Donne, John. "Meditation 17." *Devotions Upon Emergent Occasions: Together With Death's Duel.* Middlesex: The Echo Library, 2008.

—. "Anniversaries." In *The Complete Poems of John Donne.* Edited by Roger E. Bennett. Chicago: Packard and Company, 1942.

Franz, Marie-Luise von. *Psyche and Matter.* Shambhala Publications, 1992.

Frye, Roland Mushat. *The Renaissance Hamlet: Issues and Responses in 1600*. Princeton: Princeton University Press, 1984.

Holie Bible, Bishops'. 1572. Matthew Parker. Imprinted by Richarde Jugge, Printer to the Queenes Majestie. London: 1572. (Accessed in the Rare Book and Manuscript Library, Columbia University in the City of New York.)

Hume, Martin. *The Great Lord Burghley; A Study in Elizabethan Statecraft.* New York: Longmans, Green, 1898.

Jonson, Ben. "To the memory of my beloved, the author Mr. William Shakespeare" from The First Folio, 1623.

Marx, Steven. *Shakespeare and the Bible*. Oxford: Oxford University Press, 2000.

Melville, Herman. *Journal Up the Straits: October 11, 1856–May 5, 1857.* Edited by Raymond M. Weaver. New York: Colophon, 1935.

Milton, John. *Paradise Lost.* Edited by Scott Elledge. New York: W. W. Norton & Company, 1993.

Nashe, Thomas. *Summer's Last Will and Testament.* In *The Works of Thomas Nashe.* Edited by Ronald B. McKerrow. Oxford: Basil Blackwell, 1958.

Nicholl, Charles. *The Chemical Theatre.* London: Routledge & Kegan Paul, 1980.

Pagel, Walter. *Paracelsus: An Introduction to Philosophical Medicine in the Era of the Renaissance.* New York: Karger, 1982.

Shakespeare, William. *Twelfth Night; Or What You Will.* Edited by Roger Warren and Stanley Wells. Oxford: Oxford University Press, 2008.

—. *King Lear.* Edited by Grace Ioppolo. New York: W. W. Norton & Company, 2007.

—. *Hamlet, Prince of Denmark.* Edited by David Bevington and David Scott Kastan. New York: Bantam Classic, 2005.

—. *Henry IV, Part 2.* Edited by Norman N. Holland and Sylvan Barnet. New York: Signet Classic, 2002.

Shapiro, James. *A Year in the Life of William Shakespeare, 1599.* New York: Columbia University Press, 2005.

Thompson, Stephen Paul. "Shakespeare and the Elizabethan St. Paul." Dissertation, University of Iowa, 1990.

Tynan, Kenneth. *He That Plays the King: A View of the Theatre.* New York: Longmans, Green, 1950.

Van Doren, Mark. *The Autobiography of Mark Van Doren.* New York: Greenwood Press, 1968.

Winstanley, Lilian. "Hamlet and the Essex Conspiracy, Part II." *Aberystwyth Studies* 7: 37–50, 1925.

—. "Hamlet and the Essex Conspiracy."*Aberystwyth Studies* 6:47–64, 1924.

—. *Hamlet and the Scottish Succession.* Cambridge: Cambridge University Press, 1921.